Exploring the fascinating life of Jesus

Exploring the fascinating life of Jesus

— from Matthew to John
in ten minutes a day

Roger Ellsworth

 PUBLISHING WITH A MISSION

EP BOOKS
Faverdale North, Darlington, DL3 0PH, England

web: http://www.epbooks.org
e-mail: sales@epbooks.org

EP BOOKS USA
P. O. Box 614, Carlisle, PA 17013, USA

web: http://www.epbooks.us
e-mail: usasales@epbooks.org

First published 2010

British Library Cataloguing in Publication Data available

ISBN-13   978-085234-720-1   ISBN 0-85234-720-0

Printed and bound in the UK by J F Print Ltd, Sparkford, Somerset.

The following pages are lovingly dedicated to my grandson Noah Ellsworth.

Acknowledgements

Once again I find myself deeply indebted to EP Books for allowing me to participate with them in the work of the gospel. Special thanks go to David Clark, formerly of Evangelical Press, and Jackie Friston. As always, I am grateful to my wife Sylvia for her invaluable assistance.

Contents

Introduction

Several years ago, I had a crisis of faith. The constant pounding by sceptics in the schools I attended had taken its toll. To me, the issue was never whether I would be an evangelical Christian or one of a more liberal stripe, it was whether I could be a Christian at all. I was much vexed in those days about the faith that I had held since childhood. As I look back, I realize that it was not I who was holding faith; it was rather faith that was holding me.

In particular, the one issue that held me was the Gospel accounts of the life and ministry of Jesus Christ. I could not get around the evidence for him. I found him to be the inescapable Christ. The only conclusion that made sense to me was that he was God in human flesh. His miraculous deeds and his powerful and astounding teachings, all of which were substantiated by numerous witnesses, left me no room to manoeuvre. I had tried to get away from him, but he had pursued and conquered me.

I still do not have all the answers that I would like. I am not a Christian because Christianity answers all my questions. I am a Christian because Christianity gives me answers that I cannot refute. Somewhere along life's journey, it occurred to me that the truth about Jesus is so strong and compelling that I could safely put my questions in my hip pocket until I enter heaven's glory. There in his presence, I expect to finally have the answers, and that they will all make perfect sense. I also expect to feel no little embarrassment over allowing such things to trouble me.

The one thing I cannot do is go through life ignoring the truth about Jesus. My questions can wait. My confession of faith in him cannot.

The following chapters are not written for scholars and academics. They are rather for those who have not made up their minds about Jesus, and for those, like me, who have. My hope is that those in the first group will come to the truth about the Lord Jesus Christ and that those in the second group will have any lingering doubts dissolved and chilled hearts warmed. I want all those who read these lines to come away with a greater sense of awe over the incomparable, inescapable Christ and with a firmer determination to live for his glory.

I trust that by the grace of God I have learned to believe my beliefs and doubt my doubts, and I believe in Jesus. I believe that he, the second person of the Trinity, became a human being without giving up his deity. I believe that he lived without sin. I believe that he died a special kind of death, one such as no one before or since has died. I believe that on the cross he received the wrath of God in my stead so that I never have to experience that wrath myself. I believe that he arose from the dead and lives today to make intercession for his people. I believe that he gave the Holy Spirit to his people to guide, comfort, strengthen and encourage them. I believe that I will see him when he comes again and will marvel at the sight of his nail-pierced hands and wounded side. I believe that I will be made like him and will in the ceaseless ages of eternity be lost in wonder, love and praise. Yes, I believe in Jesus.

1.

The birth of Jesus

Luke 2:1-20

The prelude to the birth (vv. 1-5)

What a remarkable thing this is! Caesar is sitting on his throne in Rome without any thought at all about tiny Bethlehem in the land of Judah. It is doubtful that he had even heard of the place! He certainly had no thought about God stepping into human history. As far as he was concerned, he was God!

But as he sat there, he suddenly thought that he really ought to register everyone in his kingdom. Only then could he be assured that he would collect all the taxes that should come to him. So it was decided! Everyone would register! There are, of course, different ways to register people. The simplest way would be to have people register in the places where they were living, but, no, Caesar didn't want it done that way. Everyone must go to his home town to register! That required Joseph and

Mary to go to Bethlehem, the very place that the Old Testament promised would be the birthplace of the Messiah (Micah 5:2).

How did all this come to Caesar Augustus? Why did he decide to do this registering? Why did he decide to do it in this way? Why did he decide to do it at this time? God put it all into his head. Solomon writes:

> The king's heart is in the hand of the LORD,
> Like the rivers of water;
> He turns it wherever He wishes
>
> (Prov. 21:1).

The birth itself (vv. 6-7)

The fact that Mary's pregnancy came to full term while she and Joseph were in Bethlehem is no coincidence. In God's world, there are no coincidences, only providences.

Jesus was born while she and Joseph were in Bethlehem. His birth wove into a beautiful tapestry the divergent threads of awesome divinity and amazing humility. The former is seen in the fulfilment of prophecies. Jesus was born in Bethlehem! Jesus was a descendant of David!

The latter is seen in that he was born in a lowly stable in lowly Bethlehem. The second person of the Trinity has stooped to the lowliest of the low!

The announcement of the angel (vv. 8-12)

The assurance (vv. 8-10)

It is easy to see why the shepherds needed assurance. There they were, in the midst of what seemed to be nothing more than just another ordinary, boring night in the life of a shepherd. Suddenly

TIME OUT

◇◇◇◇◇◇◇◇◇◇◇◇◇◇◇◇◇◇◇◇◇◇◇◇◇◇◇

It is important that we remember that Jesus' life did not begin when he was conceived in his mother's womb. The Bible teaches that he was God before he came to this world. His conception and birth were not his beginning. They merely constituted the eternal God taking unto himself our humanity.

It is also crucial for us to remember that the birth of Jesus fulfilled many prophecies of the Old Testament:

- the nature of his birth — Isaiah 7:14 (Matt. 1:23)
- the place of his birth — Micah 5:2 (Luke 2:1-5)
- the worship of the Magi — Isaiah 49:7 (Matt. 2:1-12)
- the flight into Egypt — Hosea 11:1 (Matt. 2:13-15)
- the slaughter of infants — Jeremiah 31:15 (Matt. 2:16-18)

an angel appeared, with the glory of God himself shining all around him! This is not the type of thing that makes one yawn and throw another log on the fire! This sight terrified them! So the angel first allayed their fears by telling them he had come to bring 'good tidings of great joy' (v. 10).

The core of his announcement (v. 11)

- 'Saviour' means he is the deliverer of his people. Most of the Jews automatically equated deliverance with liberation from the bondage of Rome, but the Bible is quite clear that Jesus came to deliver people from their sins (Matt. 1:21).

- 'Christ' means 'anointed One'. It designates Jesus as the promised Messiah. In the Old Testament, the word 'anointed' is applied to three distinct offices. Priests were anointed with holy oil (Lev. 3:3-5,16). Prophets were called 'My anointed ones' (Ps. 105:15). And the king of Israel was called on various occasions his 'anointed' (1 Sam. 2:10,35). Jesus' ministry encompassed each of these offices. In his preaching, he performed the work of the prophet, representing God to men. In his death on the cross, he performed the work of priest, representing men to God. And he is even now at the right hand of the Father from where he rules and reigns over all those who believe.

• 'Lord' means 'master' or 'exalted One'. Jesus is Lord over all by virtue of his own person. He is God himself and, therefore, has authority over all.

A sign (v. 12)

There must have been many babies in Bethlehem that night. How were the shepherds to know which baby was the one spoken of by the angel? The final part of the angel's announcement consists of a sign: 'You will find a Babe wrapped in swaddling clothes, lying in a manger' (v. 12). Out of all the babies in Bethlehem that night, only one would be found in a lowly stable, lying in a manger!

The anthem of the heavenly host (vv. 13-14)

The announcement of the single angel caused a whole host of angels to burst into this song of adoring praise: 'Glory to God in the highest, and on earth peace, good will toward men!'

Most people are quite ready and willing to embrace the last half of this song. But start talking to them about the first part of this angelic strain and they begin to get nervous and fidgety. They like the peace and the good will, but they don't want to bow before God and say, 'Glory to God in the highest.'

Yet Christmas means God has done something. It means he has sent the Saviour. And if we are to have peace on earth and good will toward men, we must have the Saviour. The great tragedy of our day is that people want what the Saviour can provide without embracing the Saviour. But the two cannot be separated. It has often been pointed out that we cannot have peace without the Prince of Peace.

The response of the shepherds (vv. 15-20)

Try to picture yourself being with those shepherds that night. Suppose you had heard the one angel announce the birth of Jesus and all the other angels burst into praise? What would you have done? You certainly would not have fluffed up your pillow and gone to sleep! Surely, you would have done the same thing those shepherds did: they went to see the baby (vv. 15-16), they shared the good news of Jesus with all they met (vv. 17-18) and they praised and glorified God for all they had seen and heard (v. 20).

PAUSE TO REFLECT

Should you not be doing the same as the shepherds? Although you were not there that night to hear the song of the angels, it has come down through the years of time to sound again. You must do, then, as the shepherds did. Seek the Saviour. Don't rest until you have found him and made him your Lord and Saviour. And then tell others about the Saviour you have found. And don't forget to praise the God of heaven for sending such a Saviour to this sinful world.

The meaning of Christmas is settled. It isn't our place to debate and dispute it, but, by God's grace, to receive and rejoice in it.

2.
The boy Jesus in the temple

◇◇◇

Luke 2:41-52

This is the only record we have of the boyhood of Jesus. All is left in obscurity except this one episode. When Jesus was only twelve, his parents, having mistakenly assumed he was in their caravan, rushed back to Jerusalem to find him engaged in conversation with the learned teachers of the day.

We all get a good chuckle when young children put their parents on the spot. We laugh when a child knows more about something than adults. But we must not think that Luke included this incident to make us smile.

This episode is here to set before us two important things about Jesus: his astonishing nature and his overriding priority.

The astonishing nature of Jesus

Having gone with his parents to Jerusalem to observe the Passover, Jesus goes to the temple, engages the foremost scholars in deep conversation about the things of God, and leaves them amazed.

The fact that he was able to amaze the scholars with his questions and answers is an early indication that Jesus was not just another boy. How are we to explain him? The Bible leaves no room for manoeuvre here. The only explanation, as we have noted, is that he was both fully God and fully man at one and the same time, without any conflict or contradiction between the two.

What a marvel is this plan of redemption! God is in a twelve-year-old boy! A boy is both God and boy!

The marvel of Jesus deepens when we read that he increased in wisdom (v. 52). How are we to square the understanding Jesus showed at the temple with his increase in wisdom?

Matthew Poole offers this word of explanation:

If any ask how he, who was the eternal Wisdom of the Father (who is the only one wise God), increased in wisdom, they must know that all things in Scripture which are spoken of Christ, are not spoken with respect to his entire person, but with respect to the one or other nature united in that person; he increased in wisdom, as he did in age, or stature, with respect to his human, not to his Divine nature.[1]

TIME OUT

◇◇◇◇◇◇◇◇◇◇◇◇◇◇◇◇◇◇◇◇◇◇◇◇◇◇◇◇◇◇◇◇

It is estimated that sixty billion people have occupied planet earth. That's a lot of people!

One person stands out in this mass of humanity — Jesus of Nazareth.

- Jesus is the one who has divided history (B.C. & A.D.);
- Although Jesus himself never wrote a book, he has been the subject of more books than anyone else in history. The accounts of his life (the Gospels) have themselves been translated into more than 2000 languages;
- Jesus never painted a picture or wrote a poem but he has inspired more artistry than anyone else;
- Jesus never led an army, but millions have laid down their lives for him. I am not referring to those who died in wars that were mistakenly conducted in the name of Christianity, but rather to those who have died as a result of persecution (one estimate is that 330,000 die each year for their faith in Christ);
- Jesus had no formal education, but thousands of schools and universities have been founded in his name;
- Jesus never owned a building, but countless numbers of buildings have been erected in his name;
- Jesus' ministry was confined to a tiny country, but his name is known around the world.[2]

How are we to explain the enormous influence of Jesus? The Bible does not leave us in suspense about the answer. It tells us that he was no ordinary man. Its clear and unrelenting testimony is that Jesus was God in human flesh. No one ever spoke like Jesus. No one ever did the things that Jesus did. No one ever prompted deeper affection and devotion. No one ever prompted more hatred and opposition.

And Jesus is the Saviour. Out of all the billions who have lived, Jesus is the only person who can deliver people from their sins and grant them entrance into eternal glory in heaven.

Given the awesome greatness of Jesus, is it not shocking that more people are not interested in him? Is it not utterly astounding that so many are quite content to walk through life without giving Jesus careful consideration?

The overriding priority of Jesus

When Joseph and Mary found him in the temple, Mary rebuked him: 'Son, why have You done this to us? Look, Your father and I have sought You anxiously' (v. 48).

Jesus responded: 'Why did you seek Me? Did you not know that I must be about My Father's business?' (v. 49).

That 'must' tells us that he was already conscious of being on a divine mission — the Father's business!

The Father's business! This is the business of the redemption of sinners. It is the business that was planned before the world began by the Father, the Son and the Holy Spirit. This business required the Son to come to this earth as a human being. It required him to live in perfect obedience to the law of God. It required him to go to the cross of Calvary and there receive the wrath of God in the place of sinners.

This is the business that required Jesus to act as the surety for all believers, to stand in their stead and to do all for them that they could not possibly do for themselves.

While we are on this matter of the Father's business, let me say that while we do not have the same business that Jesus had, we all have business for God. Are we doing it?

> Only one life,
> 'Twill soon be past;
> Only what's done for Christ
> Will last.

PAUSE TO REFLECT

This passage calls us to see ourselves in Joseph and Mary. There is no way to get around it, they were wrong to respond to this situation as they did.

The boy Jesus in the temple

We must always remember that they were not in the dark about Jesus. Before Jesus was born, they each received special information about him from angels. They knew that he was God in flesh (Matt. 1:23; Luke 1:35). They knew that he came to provide salvation for sinners (Matt. 1:23).

Because of his special nature and the special work he came to do, there was no need for them to be concerned about his safety. There was no need for them to regard him as if he were nothing more than another child.

But did not Jesus disobey them? No! There is no word at all about his parents giving Jesus a direct order that he refused to obey. The problem arose from them assuming something that they should not have assumed.

Joseph and Mary allowed their anxieties to override their knowledge. They let worry overshadow faith! R. C. Sproul writes: 'Jesus was not only Mary and Joseph's son, He was also Mary and Joseph's Lord. In one sense Mary and Joseph's anxiety demonstrated unbelief in the revealed nature of their son.'[3]

The knowledge they had should have compelled Joseph and Mary to accommodate themselves to Jesus, but they assumed that he would accommodate them.

This passage is here to get us to see ourselves in Joseph and Mary. They were made out of the same stuff that we all share. Their error has been around for a long time and it is still around. Let me say it again: their error was wanting Jesus to accommodate them instead of them accommodating him!

Many think God should accommodate us at several points. Because we do not like to be told that there is only one way of salvation, we want God to say that there are many ways. Because we cannot tolerate the idea that salvation is provided through a man dying on a cross, we want God to offer something that is more sophisticated and less offensive.

Because we want to be able to embrace the thinking and doing of our culture, we want God to relax his call for holy living. It is the mistake of Joseph and Mary again. Because we do not want to accommodate God, he must accommodate us.

If we insist on going through life with this mentality, we shall find ourselves at odds with God in eternity.

3.
The Trinity at the Jordan

Matthew 3:13-17

This passage brings before us a remarkable sight. Here we have Jesus of Nazareth standing alongside John the Baptist in the water of the Jordan River.

That doesn't sound so remarkable. Many Jewish men were coming for John's baptism in those days.

But Jesus, while a real man, was much more than a man. He was also God.

John the Baptist knew this. He had hailed Jesus as 'the Lamb of God who takes away the sin of the world' (John 1:29).

That phrase was no accident. It was no mere flight of poetic imagination. By calling Jesus the Lamb of God, John was quite clearly and explicitly affirming that Jesus was the fulfilment of the promise God had given centuries before.

In particular, John was linking Jesus to the Passover lamb that the children of Israel had to slay. That lamb had to be without spot or blemish.

In declaring Jesus to be the Lamb of God, John was not only saying that this was the one who had come to lay down his life as the payment for the sins of his people, but also that he was spotless and without blemish (a truth repeated by the apostle Peter in 1 Peter 1:19).

The Son's baptism

Now John the Baptist had a problem on his hands. Standing here beside him in the Jordan River was the sinless one, and the baptism that he, John, was practising was one of repentance. In other words, those who submitted to it were indicating that they recognized their sinful condition and were truly repenting. But Jesus had no sin and would not seem, therefore, to have any need of baptism.

Realizing all this, John says to Jesus, 'I need to be baptized by You, and are You coming to me?' (v. 14).

It is interesting that Jesus in no way disagreed with John. We look in vain if we look for a single instance of Jesus ever acknowledging any personal sin. But while he accepted John's conclusion, he still insisted on being baptized. Why?

Jesus explains by simply saying, 'Permit it to be so now, for thus it is fitting for us to fulfill all righteousness' (v. 15).

What was he saying? Essentially this: 'John, you must yield to me on this matter because baptism is one of the Father's righteous requirements for my mission.'

Baptism was, then, part of the plan that God the Father and God the Son worked out before time began. That plan consisted of the Father giving the Son a people, and the Son agreeing to redeem them from sin by coming as their substitute and receiving the penalty due on account of their sin.

Jesus had no sin of his own, but he had to take the sins of those people. By standing there in those baptismal waters with

John, he was publicly identifying himself with his people in their sin.

I suggest that Jesus, by taking his place there with John, was for all practical purposes saying to the Father, 'I have come to stand in the place of those people you have given me. I freely and gladly identify with them in their sin so I can serve as their substitute and pay their penalty.'

TIME OUT

'It was right that he who had promised to offer himself as a ransom for many ratify this promise by means of submitting to baptism, thereby reaffirming his desire and decision to take upon himself the sin of the world. The water of baptism signifies and seals the washing away of sin, and Jesus by means of this sacrament reveals himself as the Sin-bearer. Accordingly, it was also right that John, who was fulfilling his task in obedience to God and in fulfillment of prophecy, should baptize Jesus.'[1]

The Father's response

It is not surprising to read, then, that the Father responded from heaven with these words: 'This is My beloved Son, in whom I am well pleased' (v. 17).

That was an expression of the Father's satisfaction with his Son identifying himself with sinners.

We can easily fall into the trap of thinking salvation has to satisfy us. Many hear the historic Christian gospel preached, and they begin to pronounce judgement on various aspects of it. They hear one doctrine and say they cannot accept it. They hear another and complain that it doesn't seem fair. On and on they go, believing themselves to be competent arbiters of what is right about this old gospel and what is wrong.

The consumer mentality has come to church these days, and the consumers feel as much at ease in choosing one doctrine and dispensing with another as they would if they were standing before a smorgasbord.

Many churches have decided the course of wisdom is to go with the tide. This was evidenced by a national advertising campaign undertaken a few years ago by a denomination that featured a parishioner saying, 'Instead of trying to fit a religion, I found one to fit me.'

Against all this stands the unwavering testimony of Holy Scripture that it is God who has to be satisfied before any of us can ever hope to stand in his presence. He is the one who created us for himself. He is the sovereign Lord who has the right to require his creatures to obey his commands. He is the holy and righteous one who is insulted by the stubborn refusal of his creatures to obey his commands. And for those creatures to assume that salvation must somehow or another satisfy them is rather like asking the fox to guard the chickens or the inmates to run the prison.

The thing that ought to amaze and astonish us is that this holy God whom we have so grievously insulted with our sins can ever be satisfied at all. The good news of the Christian message is not only that he *can* be satisfied, but also that he *has* been satisfied because of that man who stood there alongside John the Baptist in the water of the Jordan River. By identifying with sinners there and going to Calvary's cross and receiving their penalty, he has indeed satisfied the just claims of the holy, sovereign God. The point we need to keenly feel is this: if God is satisfied with Jesus, we had better be, as well.

The Spirit's anointing

Another dimension of Jesus' baptism must not escape our notice. Just before the Father spoke his words of approval of his

Son, the Spirit of God descended upon the Lord Jesus in the form of a dove.

The Holy Spirit, the third person of the Trinity, was at one with the Father and the Son in the plan of redemption. The Father gave a people to the Son. The Son purchased this people through his atoning death. And the Holy Spirit anoints the Son for the task and applies his atoning death to those whom the Father gave the Son.

The emphasis at this point is on the anointing the Holy Spirit bestowed upon Jesus for the work God the Father had given him to do. That work can be divided into three parts or offices: prophet, priest and king.

As prophet, Jesus was to represent God to men, faithfully proclaiming his truth to them. As priest, he offered to God the perfect sacrifice for the sins of his people — himself! As king, he rules over his people, provides for them and protects them.

This threefold office of the Lord Jesus Christ is an essential part of the redemptive work assigned to him by the Father. There can be no salvation for anyone apart from these three offices.

The sinner is ignorant of God's truth and, therefore, needs someone to instruct him. The Lord Jesus, as prophet, provides this.

The sinner is also alienated from God and needs reconciliation. By his death on Calvary's cross, Jesus took the penalty of our sin and thereby removed the barrier between God and us.

The sinner is also possessed of a nature that is stubborn and rebellious and also weak and foolish in the business of living. As king, the Lord Jesus subdues and rules the sinful nature of his people, as well as protects and guides them.

Christopher Wordsworth captured the significance of the Spirit's anointing by saying of the Lord Jesus,

Manifest at Jordan's stream,
Prophet, Priest, and King supreme.

Jesus identifies with sinners. The Father approves. And the Spirit anoints. Our redemption is the result of the triune God at work. It is the completed product of a united Godhead.

PAUSE TO REFLECT

The author of Hebrews refers to 'so great a salvation' (Heb. 2:3). Why is it so great? It was planned by God the Father, God the Son and God the Holy Spirit. Springing from eternity past, it has coursed through human history and picked up mere human specks, and will finally deposit them on the shore of heaven. We should not ask if salvation is great. We should rather ask if it is great to us.

4.

Power over temptation

◇◇◇◇◇◇◇◇◇◇◇◇◇◇◇◇◇◇◇◇◇◇◇◇◇◇◇◇◇◇◇◇◇◇◇◇◇◇◇

Luke 4:1-13

Each of the Synoptic Gospels contains an account of the temptations. Matthew and Luke go into detail about them, while Mark is content to allude to them only briefly. It should be noted that Luke gives the temptations in a different order to Matthew, but this in no way amounts to a contradiction.

It cannot be stressed too strongly that these temptations did not come to Jesus by chance. This is made clear by each of the Gospel accounts. Matthew says, 'Then Jesus was led up by the Spirit into the wilderness to be tempted by the devil' (Matt. 4:1).

Mark states it more forcefully: 'Immediately the Spirit drove Him into the wilderness' (Mark 1:12).

Luke joins Matthew in saying Jesus was 'led' by the Spirit (v. 1).

These verses help us put the temptation of Jesus in the right perspective. If we are not careful we can have a picture of Jesus as a poor victim of circumstances and see the plan of redemption tottering on the cliff of disaster.

A false reading of this passage makes Satan the challenger and has us wondering if Jesus will be able to stand up against his assault. But it was Jesus who was doing the challenging. Jesus went into the wilderness for the express purpose of encountering Satan and defeating him.

These temptations should not be viewed as tests to see if Jesus would sin, but rather as opportunities to prove that he would not. When tyre manufacturers put their tyres on a truck, hoist it in the air, and drop it, it is not to see if the tyres will blow out, but to prove that they won't.

The temptation to doubt God's Word (vv. 2-4)

Satan's argument (vv. 2-3)

We cannot properly understand this temptation if we do not connect it with what God the Father had said at Jesus' baptism, 'You are My beloved Son; in You I am well pleased' (3:22).

Now after forty days in the wilderness, Satan challenges Jesus at that point: 'If You are the Son of God, command this stone to become bread' (v. 3).

In other words, Satan was asking if that voice from heaven could be trusted. It did not appear so. If God had really declared that Jesus was his Son, why would Jesus now be hungry in the wilderness? Would God take care of his Son in such a way? If Jesus was indeed God's Son, it was clear that he did not care for him. Either God had not spoken or God was not good.

It is worth noting that Satan began with Eve in the very same way. God had allowed Adam and Eve to eat of every tree in the Garden of Eden except the tree of the knowledge of good and evil. Satan attacked at that point by saying, 'Has God indeed said, "You shall not eat of every tree of the garden"?' (Gen. 3:1).

His insinuation was clear. The Word of God could not be trusted. If God had really spoken to them, he would have allowed them to eat from all the trees. Again, either God had not spoken or he was not good.

Jesus' response (v. 4)

Jesus fended off Satan's assault by quoting the words of Deuteronomy 8:3: 'Man shall not live by bread alone, but by every word of God.'

By quoting this verse, Jesus demonstrated his complete trust in the Word of God. He did not need any other confirmation to know the Word of God was true and that his Father was good.

TIME OUT

∞∞∞∞∞∞∞∞∞∞∞∞∞∞∞∞∞∞∞∞

There are many reasons to believe the Bible is the Word of God:

- the unity of its message, although written by widely different men over centuries of time;
- its fulfilled prophecies;
- its survival against persistent and vicious attacks;
- the changed lives of those who believe and obey it.

But the main reason to believe the Bible is this: Jesus believed it.

- he explicitly affirmed its authority;
- he endorsed those sections that are often questioned;
- he appealed to it to settle disputes and controversies.

The temptation to resist God's will (vv. 5-8)

Satan's argument (vv. 5-7)

In this temptation Satan gave Jesus a panoramic view of all the kingdoms of the world. The emphasis was on the splendour, the beauty, the desirability of these kingdoms; that is, how they appealed to the eye.

Satan was clearly seeking to excite the affections of Jesus and entice him to put them above everything else. He was seeking to get Jesus to disobey what he knew to be the truth of God. God's will was for Jesus to have dominion through his death on the cross. But Satan tried to destroy Jesus' commitment to that truth by offering him dominion without him having to travel the pathway of the cross.

Jesus' response (v. 8)

Jesus warded off this temptation by drawing from Deuteronomy 6:13: 'You shall worship the LORD your God, and Him only you shall serve.'

Given the opportunity to renounce the Father who sent him and the cross to which he was sent, the Lord Jesus Christ powerfully affirmed both.

The temptation to test God's love (vv. 9-12)

Satan's argument (vv. 9-11)

This temptation seems to have been the most subtle and treacherous of the three because Satan here shifts his ground. In other words, he seizes what Jesus had already established in the first two temptations — that he, Jesus, trusted the Father's

Word, the Father's love, and was committed to the Father's mission — to frame this temptation.

Here Satan also resorts to Scripture and essentially says, 'It is obvious that you love God the Father very much and he loves you very much. I know a way in which you can demonstrate how much you love God and how much he loves you. Leap from the pinnacle of the temple.'

Jesus' response (v. 12)

Jesus answered this temptation by quoting Deuteronomy 6:16: 'You shall not tempt the LORD your God.'

Those who trust in God's love do not put him to the test. They do not say, ' If God really loves me, he will heal me of this disease, give me that promotion, let me marry that person...'

God's people trust God's love, not because God orders their circumstances in the way they would like, but because he has firmly declared his love for his people in his Word and has decisively demonstrated it on Calvary's cross.

For a Christian to put God's love to the test by insisting that he do one thing or the other is not trust at all. We only test what we doubt. The man who knows his brakes will work doesn't keep tapping the pedal. In like manner, if Jesus had leapt off the temple, he would not have been showing that he trusted the Father's love but rather that he doubted it.

This teaching seems to fly in the face of God's Word to the people of Malachi's day: '"Bring all the tithes into the storehouse, that there may be food in My house, and try Me now in this," says the LORD of hosts, "if I will not open for you the windows of heaven and pour out for you such blessing that there will not be room enough to receive it"' (Mal. 3:10).

We may answer this dilemma by saying there is all the difference in the world between trying God when he commands it and trying him when he has not commanded it. The passage in

Malachi should probably be understood as a special invitation from God to his people to stir them to greater faith in an age of unusual scepticism and doubt.

PAUSE TO REFLECT
◇◇◇◇◇◇◇◇◇◇◇◇◇◇◇◇◇◇◇◇◇◇◇◇◇◇◇◇◇◇◇◇◇◇◇◇◇◇◇

1. The temptations were an essential part of Jesus' saving work. Satan had succeeded in his temptations of the first head of the human race, Adam, but another Adam was on the scene now as the representative head of redeemed humanity. The Father sends him into the wilderness and essentially says to Satan, 'Let's see how you do with this Adam!'

   To die for the sins of others, Christ, the new Adam, had to be free from sin. Had he sinned himself, he would have had to pay the penalty for his own sin and could not, therefore, have paid for the sins of anyone else.

2. The temptations of Jesus were essentially the same as those Satan used with Eve in the Garden of Eden.

3. The devil is a real person who diligently opposes the cause of God and the people of God.

4. Our most effective weapon for resisting Satan's temptations is the Word of God (Eph. 6:17; Heb. 4:12)

5. Because the Lord Jesus was tempted, he can sympathize with his people when they are tempted (Heb. 2:18; 4:14-16).

5.

A question that was

<><><><><><><><><><><><><><><><><><><><><><><><><>

never answered

<><><><><><><><><><><><><><><><><><><><><><>

John 1:43-51

The passage before us enables us to see the special nature of Jesus once again. Here we have Jesus calling Nathanael to be his disciple.

A message that still applies

One day, as Nathanael was sitting under a fig tree, his friend Philip suddenly burst upon him with these words: 'We have found Him of whom Moses in the law, and also the prophets, wrote — Jesus of Nazareth, the son of Joseph.'

This was a monumental announcement. Generation after generation had come and gone, and God's promised Saviour had not come. But now Philip is standing before Nathanael saying, 'We have found Him'!

The happy message Philip announced on this occasion has not been withdrawn. It was good news on that day, and it is still good news today. The Christ whom Philip found came to provide eternal salvation by dying on the cross, and that salvation is still available today.

A mindset that still exists

We would like to think that Nathanael responded to Philip's news by leaping to his feet and joyfully shouting: 'Show me the way!' But he did not. The news Philip announced must have sounded like a beautiful melody in his ears until he got to that part about Nazareth. That word interrupted the melody with a dreadful clang.

Perhaps Nathanael was thinking of the prophecy of Micah which says that the Messiah will be born in Bethlehem (Micah 5:2). Perhaps he assumed the glorious Messiah could not possibly come from a town as unappealing as Nazareth.

Whatever flashed through his mind, it was sufficient for him to conclude that Philip was mistaken. This Jesus might be very wonderful and special, but he could not be the Messiah. It was simply inconceivable. Nathanael could not at this point accept the message because he had a preconceived notion that ruled it out.

Nathanael was not the last to have a predisposition against the truth. Let someone proclaim the good news that forgiveness of sins and eternal life in heaven are available in Christ, and many, because of their bias against the truth, will rule it out before even listening to the evidence. They say, 'Eternal salvation through a Jewish rabbi dying on a Roman cross two thousand years ago? The thing is ridiculous. It is simply inconceivable. No one in his right mind would believe such a message.'

To those who are in the grip of a bias against the truth, we Christians take up the words of Philip to Nathanael: 'Come and see' (v. 46). We ask you to suspend your bias long enough to come and take a hard look at the evidence for Christ.

Evidence that must still be considered

Philip's invitation was one Nathanael could not resist. Even if Jesus could not be the Messiah, it was obvious that he had made such an impression on Philip that Nathanael had to learn more about him. Scripture does not tell us what Nathanael expected to find when he encountered Jesus. His grand assumption about Nazareth certainly ruled out any expectation of finding the Messiah. But that is exactly what he found. As he and Philip approached, Jesus said to him, 'Behold, an Israelite indeed, in whom is no deceit!' (v. 47).

Nathanael's response was just what we would expect. He was a sceptical sort who would not jump to conclusions without evidence, and he could not, therefore, accept Jesus' commendation without knowing how Jesus arrived at it. 'How do You know me?' he asked (v. 48). Jesus' answer not only caught Nathanael off guard but also changed him for ever. Jesus said, 'Before Philip called you, when you were under the fig tree, I saw you' (v. 48).

Jesus' assessment of Nathanael was not just a lucky guess or unsubstantiated flattery designed to curry favour. It was based on personal knowledge. That knowledge was so extensive and penetrating that it even extended to the cover of a fig tree. There Nathanael could be hidden from the eyes of others, but he was not hidden from the Christ.

Nathanael's bias melted in the bright glare of Jesus' omniscience. He now knew the truth about Jesus, and he quickly and powerfully confessed that truth: 'Rabbi, You are the Son of God! You are the King of Israel!' (v. 49).

It is interesting that Nathanael had nothing to say about Nazareth. He still did not know how Nazareth fitted into this puzzle, but he could not allow what he did *not* know to obscure what he *did* know. This Jesus was the Messiah. There could be no other explanation for him. Nathanael could wait to find out about Nazareth, but he could not wait to confess the faith that flooded his heart.

TIME OUT

Christians believe in Christ because they have encountered overwhelming evidence that he is indeed God in human flesh.

The Gospel accounts of his penetrating insight into men, such as we have here with Nathanael, are only one such evidence (John 2:23-25; 4:17-19,29). We also have those passages that explicitly affirm that Jesus knew what lay ahead of him (Matt. 16:21; 17:22-23; 20:17-19). Then there are those episodes in which he demonstrated his power over disease (Matt. 4:23-24; 9:35; 14:34-36; Mark 1:34), nature (Mark 4:35-39) and death itself (Mark 5:41-42; Luke 7:11-15; John 11:43-44).

In addition to these we find numerous passages which demonstrate his minute fulfilment of the centuries-old prophecies of the Old Testament (e.g. Matt. 21:5,9; 27:35; see also Luke 24:27,44). The icing on the cake, so to speak, is his own resurrection from the dead.

Once one has had the big questions of the person and work of Christ answered, other questions do not seem quite so pressing and urgent.

A promise that still counts

Nathanael would have been satisfied that day had he done nothing more than meet the Messiah. But the Lord Jesus Christ had not finished with him just yet. Nathanael had owned him as the Messiah because Jesus had seen him sitting under the fig tree.

Yet that was relatively minor when compared to what Nathanael was about to see. Jesus said, 'Most assuredly, I say to you, hereafter you shall see heaven open, and the angels of God ascending and descending upon the Son of Man' (v. 51).

Jesus' terminology was not lost on Nathanael. It drew on the story of the Old Testament patriarch, Jacob. While fleeing from his brother Esau, Jacob had a vision in which he saw a ladder extending to heaven and angels ascending and descending on it. The ladder Jacob saw was only a faint glimmer of the coming Christ. He is the only true ladder between heaven and earth. Leon Morris says Jesus is 'the link' between heaven and earth and 'the means by which the realities of heaven are brought down to earth.'[1]

Nathanael and the other disciples were destined to see Jesus bringing heaven to earth. All through his ministry they would see his heavenly power and grace.

The promise the Lord Jesus gave to Nathanael is one that all Christians may claim. We have, as he did, tasted of that heavenly power and grace; but there is much more to come. The Lord Jesus even now says to all of his people, 'You will see greater things than these.' That promise will at last be fulfilled when he receives us to himself in realms of eternal glory.

If we would receive these marvellously great and wonderful things, we must, as Nathanael did, cast aside our doubts and scepticism, and embrace Christ with a true and living faith. We must join him in saying to Christ from our hearts, 'You are the Son of God! You are the King of Israel' (v. 49).

PAUSE TO REFLECT

Ours is a day in which we pride ourselves, not on our convictions, but rather on our doubts, and we frown upon those who claim to have certainty. Nothing so riles modern society as for someone to claim that there is such a thing as absolute truth and that he has found it. We don't mind people searching for truth as long as they never arrive at it.

While the winds of tolerance and pluralism are steadily blowing, let the word go out that Nathanael's heartfelt confession must be ours if we hope to enter heaven at last. No one can be saved who is not definite in his conviction about the Lord Jesus Christ. The road that leads to eternal life has a narrow gate (Matt. 7:13-14). That gate is far too narrow for anyone to enter while armed with ambiguities and uncertainties.

6.
The first sign

◇◇◇◇◇◇◇◇◇◇◇◇◇◇◇◇◇◇◇◇◇◇◇◇◇◇◇◇◇◇◇

John 2:1-11

In his account of the life of Jesus, the apostle John uses the word 'signs' for the miracles that Jesus performed (John 20:30-31).

When we hear the word 'sign', we immediately think of something that points to something else. A sign for a city is not the city itself. Furthermore, the city is greater than any of the signs that point to it.

So it was with the miracles of Jesus. They were designed to point to something beyond themselves, and the thing to which they point is greater than the miracles themselves. We are very wrong, then, to focus so much on the miracles of Jesus that we fail to see the greater things to which they point.

The passage before us relates the first sign that Jesus performed. He turned water into wine at a wedding feast in Cana. And the apostle John leaves us in no doubt about the reality to which this sign pointed. He says very plainly that this miracle 'manifested His glory; and His disciples believed in Him' (v. 11).

The disciples believed in Jesus before he performed this miracle. What we are to understand, then, is that this miracle caused them to believe even more. It confirmed for them that they were correct in their beliefs about Jesus. It strengthened and increased their faith in him.

TIME OUT

John's Gospel relates six other signs performed by Jesus:

- healing of the nobleman's son (4:46-54);
- healing of the lame man (5:1-9);
- feeding of the five thousand (6:1-14);
- stilling the storm (6:15-21);
- healing the blind man (9:1-7);
- raising Lazarus from the dead (11:38-44).

The apostle John wrote these words about the signs of Jesus: 'And truly Jesus did many other signs in the presence of His disciples, which are not written in this book; but these are written that you may believe that Jesus is the Christ, the Son of God, and that believing you may have life in His name' (20:30-31).

The thing we most need to see in Jesus is his glory

By the word 'glory', we are referring to the glory of God. When John tells us that this miracle manifested the glory of Jesus, he is telling us that this miracle revealed the glory of God in Jesus.

Jesus was no ordinary man. He was God in human flesh. His humanity was real, but there was more to him than humanity. And just when he appeared to be nothing more than another man, he would pull back the veil of that humanity so that those around him could see the underlying deity. J. C. Ryle writes: 'After thirty years' seclusion at Nazareth, He now for the first time lifted up the veil which He had thrown over His divinity in becoming flesh, and revealed something of His almighty power and Godhead.'[1]

He did it on the Mount of Transfiguration. There he appeared in heavenly glory along with Moses and Elijah. And there could be no doubt that he was God in human flesh.

The apostle John wrote this Gospel many years after Jesus was crucified, arose from the grave and ascended to the Father in heaven. And after years of thinking about all that he had seen and heard when he walked with Jesus, he offered this careful and considered conclusion: 'And the Word became flesh and dwelt among us, and we beheld His glory, the glory as of the only begotten of the Father, full of grace and truth' (John 1:14).

There can be no doubt about what John was saying. He and the other disciples had carefully studied Jesus. As they walked with him, they watched him, and as they watched him, they kept seeing things that told them that he was nothing less than God in human flesh.

We are not walking with Jesus in the same way that John and the other disciples were, but we can still see his glory. It is right here in the biblical accounts of Jesus. As we read these accounts, we see his glory, and it is the glory of God.

Nothing is more vital for the church today than to be continually seeing the glory of Jesus. The church seems to be trying to subsist on a miniature Christ rather than on the mighty, glorious Christ of Scripture. But a miniature Christ has no power to stir the church or to bless her.

The glory of Jesus is best seen in the salvation he provided by his death on the cross

This comes out very plainly in John's account. Jesus and his disciples have gone to Cana to attend a wedding feast. Jesus' mother is also there.

Everything was going along swimmingly, when disaster struck. They ran out of wine! This may not appear to be much of a calamity to us, but in those days it was such a serious matter that it was considered an ill omen for the young couple. Wine, a symbol of joy (Judges 9:13; Psalm 104:15; Ecclesiastes 10:19), was considered essential for such a happy occasion. It was no small thing, therefore, when the wine ran out.

No one else seemed to know what to do about this dilemma, but Mary knew. She reported it to Jesus in these simple words: 'They have no wine.'

Jesus responded by saying, 'Woman, what does your concern have to do with Me?' (v. 4).

We have to keep our eye on the ball here. Some people allow themselves to get sidetracked by wondering if Jesus was rude to his mother! Others fret and stew over whether the wine that Jesus made was fermented or not!

The 'ball' on which we need to keep our eye is that which we have been noticing, the glory of Christ, and, in particular, the glory of his salvation.

How did Jesus manifest the glory of his salvation here? Let's think about this. In responding to his mother, Jesus specifically said that his 'hour' had not yet come.

There can be no doubt at all about the 'hour' to which he was referring. John shows us again and again in his Gospel that this 'hour' refers to Jesus' death on the cross. Jesus came to this earth with an appointment. That appointment was with the cross. Everything he did was with that appointment in mind and designed to move him closer to it.

So Jesus was essentially saying, 'Dear lady, I will only do those things that point to my reason for coming to this earth.'

He then commanded that six waterpots be filled with water (vv. 6-7). The apostle John found particular significance in the fact that the waterpots Jesus used were for the ceremonial cleansings required by Judaism (v. 6). It was as if Jesus was exposing the inadequacy of Judaism as a religion of salvation.

The religion of Judaism stressed the keeping of the commandments of God, but the fact that no one could perfectly keep them shows that it is impossible for us to attain salvation by our own efforts.

But Jesus is more than adequate to save. There on the cross, he received the wrath of God in the place of sinners, so that all who believe in him will never have to receive that wrath themselves but are saved from it!

The fact that Jesus transformed the water in those pots indicated that what he had come to do would surpass Judaism even as wine surpasses water.

That brings us to a final consideration.

Even more of the glory of Christ will be seen in the future

When the master of the feast tasted the wine, he essentially said to the bridegroom, 'You have saved the best for last.'

While salvation offers many benefits and blessings in this world, these things cannot begin to compare to the glory that awaits believers in heaven (Romans 8:18; 2 Corinthians 4:16-18).

This led J. C. Ryle to write:

A greater marriage feast than that of Cana will one day be held, when Christ Himself will be the bridegroom and believers will be the bride. A greater glory will one day be manifested, when Jesus shall take to Himself His great power and reign. Blessed will they be in that day who are called to the marriage supper of the Lamb![2]

PAUSE TO REFLECT

All who trust in Jesus can testify to his saving power. Warren Wiersbe offers the following story:

> I am reminded of the story of the drunken coal miner who was converted and became a vocal witness for Christ. One of his friends tried to trap him by asking, 'Do you believe that Jesus turned water into wine?'
>
> 'I certainly do!' the believer replied. 'In my home, He has turned wine into furniture, decent clothes, and food for my children.'[3]

7.

Cleansing the temple

John 2:13-22

It was the Passover season, and Jesus was in Jerusalem. The Passover! Every God-fearing Jew loved it immensely. It commemorated that night long ago in Egypt, when the angel of death 'passed over' the firstborn of the nation of Israel.

The reason for this was that the Israelites had sacrificed lambs as substitutes for the firstborn and placed the blood of those lambs on their houses. All those in houses under the blood were safe from the sentence of condemnation (Exodus 11:1 - 12:30).

The Passover was, therefore, a time for the people to reflect with deep gratitude on what God had done in the past and to offer sacrifices.

TIME OUT

◇◇◇◇◇◇◇◇◇◇◇◇◇◇◇◇◇◇◇◇◇◇◇◇◇◇◇

Every Christian should understand the Jewish attachment to the Passover. We have our own — Jesus! (1 Cor. 5:7). He is the Lamb that was slain on the cross. All those who believe in him will never have to endure the wrath of God. The wrath fell on him, and now, because of him, God's judgement 'passes over' all who trust Christ.

The Passover described in this passage was not one of unmingled joy for Jesus, as it should have been. In fact, it caused him to be angry — very angry! Let's think about the action that Jesus took at this Passover and about what his action tells us about him.

The action of Jesus

The reason for this action

The Passover was also a time of terrible abuse. Because it brought thousands of pilgrims to Jerusalem, it meant that some could make a lot of money.

Many of the pilgrims would come without an animal for sacrifice. Others would bring animals only to have the inspectors find flaws that made those animals unacceptable for sacrifice. Animals were kept on hand for worshippers who needed them, but the prices were exorbitant.

Another abuse had to do with the temple tax, which had to be paid in Jewish currency. When worshippers came to Jerusalem from other lands, their currency had to be exchanged. This service was also performed at the temple, but, again, at a substantial cost.

It was quite a scene that greeted Jesus when he arrived at the outer court of the temple. Sheep were bleating and bawling. Merchants were barking out their prices. The stench of excrement was everywhere. There was nothing there to indicate or to encourage worship.

Overwhelmed with indignation and with zeal for his 'Father's house' (v. 16), Jesus made 'a whip of cords' (v. 15) and 'drove them all out of the temple' (v. 15), overturning the tables of the moneychangers in the process (v. 15).

The results of this action (vv. 17-22)

What Jesus did had an effect upon his disciples. It caused them to call to mind the words of Psalm 69:9. That verse, from one of the messianic psalms, had been fulfilled before their eyes.

His action also had an effect upon the religious leaders. It caused them to be indignant and to ask Jesus to perform a sign (vv. 18-21).

By demanding a sign, these men were asking Jesus to prove that he had the authority to do what he had done.

William Hendriksen remarks: ' ... this request was *stupid*. The temple-cleansing was itself a sign. It was a definite anticipatory fulfillment of Mal. 3:1-3 ("The Lord, whom ye seek, will suddenly come to His temple ... He will purify the sons of Levi") ...'[1]

The request for a sign was not only stupid, however; it was also wicked. It was the result of unwillingness to admit guilt. The authorities should have been ashamed of all this graft and greed within the temple-court. Instead of asking Jesus by what right he had cleansed the temple, they should have confessed their sins and thanked him.

Jesus gave them an answer that baffled them (v. 19). His authority lay in his ability to build in three days a destroyed temple!

They were astonished because they assumed he was speaking of that building which had been under construction for forty-six years. The disciples, who were taking all this in, would come to understand later that he was referring to the temple of his body, which he did raise up three days after it was destroyed, that is, after he died. A. W. Pink writes of Jesus:

> In raising Himself from the dead He would furnish the final proof that He was God manifest in flesh, and if God, then the One Who possessed the unequivocal right to cleanse the defiled temple which bore His name.[2]

The Jesus of the action

The zeal of Jesus for the temple should cause all of us to consider how much zeal we have for the church and its worship.

There are several things we can learn from this episode.

Jesus highly values worship and insists that it be done in the right way

We are living in days in which people are very, very sure of themselves, and they are never more so than when it comes to the matter of public worship. All are experts on the matter! And they have absolutely no hesitation in suggesting that some part of worship should be dropped, another part be changed and yet another part be added!

Ask them whether they have carefully studied the Scriptures on worship, and they admit that they have not. Ask them whether they have read any books by the leading evangelical theologians, and once again they have to admit that they have not. But they still feel qualified to pronounce!

When we carefully analyse and evaluate such people, we soon find the problem. They think that worship services should offer what they like! If they like country music, worship should be a country 'hoe down'!

Meanwhile, the Bible teaches that worship should offer what God likes! And he has made it plain that he does not think as we do (Isa. 55:8-9).

The biggest problem we are having in public worship is that people never 'shift gears'. They have spent the whole week in a culture that is infatuated with entertainment and which panders to the customer. So they come to church expecting to be entertained and to be accommodated.

They never seem to realize that public worship brings us into the presence of a holy and majestic God, and we should act accordingly.

We would do well to ponder Jesus cleansing the temple and to ask ourselves what he would do if he were to come into our churches? Would he drive us out because we have turned the house of God into a place of entertainment where people put themselves on display?

What is acceptable worship? It is that which is in accordance with what God has revealed — reverent and God-honouring.

Jesus has great anger as well as great mercy

Jesus is often assumed to be so sweet and cuddly that he would never harm a fly. This is a far cry from the Jesus we have in this passage — the Jesus with a whip in his hand!

This Jesus is the same one who has promised to judge all people who pass through this life without receiving him as their rightful Lord and only Saviour (John 5:22, 26-30).

Jesus claims absolute supremacy for himself

His cleansing of the temple, coupled with his promise that he would rise again, show him to be nothing less than God in human flesh. The religious leaders of that day failed to see this truth and failed to submit themselves to him. May God help us to learn from their horrible error.

PAUSE TO REFLECT

◇◇◇

Bruce Milne applies Jesus' cleansing of the temple in this way:

Modern-day worship which is irreverent, superficial, distraction-filled, cold, lifeless, sloppy, self-indulgent, hypocritical, ill-prepared or theologically inappropriate will likewise receive his censure, as will worship which detracts from the honour and glory of the living God through a concern for performance and self-display on the part of those leading it.[3]

8.

A teacher goes to night school

John 3:1-18

Nicodemus was a very intelligent and influential man. He was a Pharisee (v. 1) and a ruler of the Jews (v. 1). He was also noted and honoured as a teacher (v. 10). Because wealth usually goes hand in hand with high social standing, it is also likely that Nicodemus was quite rich.

Many think they would be happy if they could attain the stature and the standing of a man like Nicodemus, but he had all these things and was deeply dissatisfied.

Being aware of the great miracles that Jesus had been doing (v. 2), Nicodemus sought him out. We should not attach too much significance to his coming by night. It could have been that he was too busy during the day. Or it could be that he simply wanted to insure privacy. Some think he chose night because he feared being seen with Jesus.

The important thing is not why he went at night but that he went.

Jesus talks about spiritual birth (vv. 3-8)

Spiritual birth is absolutely indispensable for entering the kingdom of God (v. 3)

Jesus didn't object to Nicodemus calling him 'a teacher come from God'. He rather used the opportunity to draw his attention to the purpose for which he, Jesus, had been sent. He essentially said, 'You say I am sent from God. Let me tell you why.'

Jesus was sent to provide the way for sinners to enter heaven. Nicodemus wanted Jesus to confirm his messiahship. Nicodemus assumed that he, by virtue of being a Jew, would automatically be part of the Messiah's kingdom. Imagine his shock when he learned that Jesus' kingdom was not of this world and that one had to be born into it through a spiritual birth! Just as we have no knowledge or experience of physical life until we are born into it, so we have no knowledge or experience of spiritual life until we are born into it.

J. C. Ryle pointedly says, 'A day will come when those who are not born again will wish that they had never been born at all.'[1]

Spiritual birth can only be initiated and produced by God (vv. 3-7)

Nicodemus wondered how such a birth could take place again (vv. 3-4). William Barclay explains:

It is as if Nicodemus said with infinite, wistful yearning: 'You talk about being born again; you talk about this radical fundamental change which is so necessary. I know that it is necessary; but in my experience it is so impossible. There is nothing I would like more; but you might as well tell me, a full grown man, to enter into my mother's womb and to be born all over again.' It is not the desirability of this change that Nicodemus questioned; that he knew only too well; it is the possibility. Nicodemus is up against the eternal problem, the problem of the man who wants to be changed, and who cannot change himself.[2]

But Jesus was talking about a birth that was 'of water and the Spirit' (v. 5). Because water is used in Scripture as an emblem of the Word of God (Ps. 119:9; Eph. 5:26), we should understand that the spiritual birth is produced by the Spirit of God using the Word of God or making the teachings of God's Word effective in the heart of the unbeliever (Rom. 10:17; Eph. 6:17; James 1:18; 1 Peter 1:23).

TIME OUT

J. C. Ryle writes:

This mighty change, it must never be forgotten, we cannot give to ourselves. The very name which our Lord gives to it is a convincing proof of this. He calls it 'a birth'. No man is the author of his own existence, and no man can quicken his own soul. We might as well expect a dead man to give himself life, as expect a natural man to make himself spiritual. A power from above must be put in exercise, even that same power which created the world (2 Cor. iv.6.) Man can do many things; but he cannot give life either to himself or to others. To give life is the peculiar prerogative of God.[3]

Gordon Keddie adds:

The new birth is a secret work of God, in which the Holy Spirit works according to his hidden power and secret will. The new birth is not predictable, because it is a sovereign work of God's grace. It is not an act of the human will, because it is effected by the Holy Spirit in a heart that is opposed to the very idea. It is all the work of God.[4]

Spiritual birth results in noticeable effects (v. 8)

Just as our physical birth results in us having the nature of our parents, so spiritual birth results in us having a new nature, a spiritual nature that evidences itself just as the wind evidences itself. Some have advocated that it is possible to have spiritual life and give little or no indication of it. They contend that there are three classes of people: those who are saved, those who are unsaved and those who are saved but live as if they are unsaved. Those in the last category are called 'carnal Christians'. The word 'carnal' means 'having the nature of the flesh', 'being governed by human nature', or 'being controlled by animal appetites'.

It is true, of course, that Christians do not attain perfection in this life. Every Christian can and does act carnally at given points in his life, but that is a far cry from saying that it is possible to be a Christian and continually live in sin. The spiritual life planted in the Christian by the Spirit of God will not allow him to live in such a way (2 Cor. 5:17; James 4:4-5; 1 John 3:9 — we should understand John's phrase 'does not sin' to mean 'does not continually and habitually practise sin').

Jesus talks about himself and his mission (vv. 9-21)

He came from heaven with heaven's authority (vv. 9-13)

Jesus was not speaking as one more in a long line of religious teachers. He spoke as a reliable authority because he had firsthand knowledge of heavenly things. He had this knowledge because he came from heaven (vv. 11,13). It was impossible for Nicodemus or anyone else to ascend to heaven and secure information about the new birth, but it was not impossible for Jesus to come from heaven to earth (v. 13).

Matthew Henry notes: '...the truths of Christ are of undoubted certainty. We have all the reasons in the world to be assured that the sayings of Christ are faithful sayings, and such as we may venture our souls upon; for he is not only a credible witness, who would not go about to deceive us, but a competent witness, who could not himself be deceived.'5

He came from heaven to make spiritual birth possible (vv. 14-17)

The spiritual birth of which Jesus had been speaking could not take place apart from the completion of his mission which he would accomplish by dying on the cross. In these verses, Jesus points Nicodemus to the cross.

1. Jesus' death was designed to deal with sin (v. 14)

God commanded Moses to lift up the serpent in the wilderness as the remedy for the sin of Israel (Num. 21:4-9). Jesus would be lifted up on the cross to make atonement for sin. Spiritual birth is life that is granted to us by God himself through his Spirit and his Word. God could not grant us life until something was done about our sins. God has said from the beginning that sin brings death.

God could not simply ignore our sin. His holy character made that impossible. God has to punish sin or cease to be God. How, then, could God at one and the same time punish sinners with eternal death and yet give them spiritual and eternal life? The cross is the answer. There God punished sin in Christ and provided the way for sinners to have eternal life.

2. Jesus' death expressed the love of God (vv. 16-17)

What marvellous love is manifested by the cross of Christ! It is marvellous because it was given by an unspeakably glorious person (God), to unspeakably needy people (perishing), at an unspeakably great cost (only begotten Son), to bestow an unspeakably great benefit (everlasting life).

3. Jesus' death must be appropriated by faith (vv. 15-21)

The word 'believe' carries with it the element of commitment. It is not just agreeing that Jesus actually lived and that he died on the cross, but rather relying on him and his death for our eternal salvation.

PAUSE TO REFLECT

The entire human race is divided into two groups: those who have genuine faith in Christ and those who do not. Why are so many in this latter group? The truth about Jesus Christ shines like light, but everyone comes into this world with a nature that loves the darkness of sin. Those who love darkness cannot love light. How then can anyone come to the light? No one can, apart from God working within him and enabling him to do so. The one who comes to the light manifests or proves in the very act of coming that God has been working in him.

9.

Good news for an outcast

◇◇◇

John 4:1-38

It is very interesting that the apostle John follows his account of Nicodemus with the story of the woman from Samaria.

There could hardly be a greater difference between two people. Nicodemus was the consummate insider. He was a man of great learning, influence and wealth. But none of these things qualified him to enter the kingdom of God, and the Lord Jesus shared with him the good news of a spiritual birth that comes from God alone.

The Samaritan woman comes from the opposite end of the spectrum. She was very much an outsider. We can go further. She was an outcast of a nation of outcasts.

Verse 9 tells us that the Jews had 'no dealings' with the Samaritans. Why was this the case?

In 722 B.C., the Assyrians invaded the land of Israel and carried many of its citizens into captivity. These people, for the most part, were absorbed into Assyria and never returned.

The land of Israel, on the other hand, was populated with those who were not taken captive and with people from foreign lands whom the Assyrians brought in. It was not long before the Israelites began to inter-marry with the other people, creating a mixed race which became known as Samaritans.

In 586 B.C. the Babylonians invaded the land of Judah and carried many of her citizens into captivity. The people of Judah, unlike those of Israel, did not lose their identity. They returned to their homeland under the leadership of Ezra and Nehemiah.

When the people of Judah began to rebuild the temple in Jerusalem, the Samaritans wanted to help but were rejected. With bitterness they turned against the Jews of Jerusalem and proceeded to build their own temple on Mount Gerizim.

The hostility between the Jews and Samaritans was extremely deep-seated and very much alive during Jesus' earthly ministry.

The Samaritans had their own outcasts. The woman in this passage came to draw water at noon, a time when she could avoid contact with the other women of the city. Her reasons? She had been married five times and was now living with a man to whom she was not married. She was, therefore, an outcast of the outcasts.

Yet she was important to Jesus, and he went to Samaria to bring her the good news of the salvation he had come to provide. As he had good news for Nicodemus, the insider, so he had good news for this woman, the outsider. Let us examine how Jesus dealt with her.

Jesus arrested her attention (vv. 7-12)

He did this in a couple of ways, the first of which is that he spoke to her (vv. 7-9).

This was no small thing. No one would have raised an eyebrow about Jesus talking to Nicodemus (a Jew, a man, a religious leader, learned, wealthy, one who recognized Jesus had come from God).

But here Jesus talks not merely to a Samaritan, which was shocking in and of itself, but to a woman who was an adulteress, ignorant, poor, and who had no idea about the identity of the one speaking to her. Isn't it interesting that while Jesus talked to Nicodemus at night, he talked to this woman in broad daylight?

The second way in which Jesus arrested her attention was by speaking to her about 'living water' (vv. 10-15). When this woman came to the well, Jesus approached her in terms of the physical ('Give Me a drink'), but he quickly moved to the spiritual ('living water'). It took a while for the woman to realize that Jesus was talking about a different kind of water than that which she could draw (vv. 11-12).

Like this woman, many think exclusively in terms of the here and now. They look upon Christianity as nothing more than another way to help them cope with the challenges of life. They fail to realize that their basic need is spiritual in nature and that Christianity deals with that need. Those who stay focused on this life and the needs of the moment will never come to salvation. J. C. Ryle notes:

> Riches, and rank, and place, and power, and learning, and amusements, are utterly unable to fill the soul. He that only drinks of these waters is sure to thirst again.[1]

Salvation is appropriately symbolized by water because it cleanses the soul as water cleanses the body. Furthermore, salvation:

1. places a new principle within us (v. 14). It is not a matter of merely adding religious activities to our lives. It means an inner transformation has taken place;

2. continues throughout this life and finally issues in eternal life (v. 14).

The water of salvation springs unceasingly from a fountain that is placed within. Whoever truly receives Christ as Lord and Saviour will never be able to get away from it. Salvation will always be at work in his life, and when this life is over he will be ushered into eternal life.

Jesus revealed her need for spiritual cleansing (vv. 15-24)

He also did this by showing to her two things.

The reality of sin in her life (vv. 15-18)

The woman had obviously failed to conform to God's commandments. She had gone from husband to husband, totalling five. The implication is that she had violated God's laws on divorce. She was now living with a man who was not her husband, a clearcut violation of God's demand for sexual morality.

Her failure to worship God (vv. 19-24)

Uncomfortable with Jesus' words about her sin, the woman quickly tried to change the subject to one of the most controversial topics of the day — the proper place to worship (v. 20). This is still a favourite strategy among those who are faced with their sins!

The woman's strategy only succeeded in opening the door for Jesus to press upon her the reality of her need. Out of aversion toward the Jews, the Samaritans had, without divine sanction, built their own temple upon a site that they had chosen, that is, Mount Gerizim. They had constructed their own religion.

TIME OUT

◇◇◇◇◇◇◇◇◇◇◇◇◇◇◇◇◇◇◇◇◇◇◇◇◇

'...the Samaritan religion was a man-made religion, and Jesus would not allow the Samaritan woman to believe that any religion of human origin, a religion based on human ideas is acceptable to Jehovah... Accordingly, salvation was of the Jews alone because only the Jews possessed a religion that had its origin in God. Moreover, it was only in Judaism, with its system of sacrifices and temple worship, that there was any true sense of the holiness of God and of the necessity of a substitutionary sacrifice as the grounds of forgiveness and of an acceptable approach to Him.'[2]

The Jewish religion, on the other hand, was based on divine revelation. All who were saved had to embrace through faith the saving truth that God had revealed to the Jews.

The controversy between the Samaritans and Jews on the proper place for worship was about to be rendered meaningless because the Messiah to whom the temple and all its rituals pointed had arrived in the person of Jesus. Through the salvation provided by Jesus, God would seek and find people to worship him wholeheartedly with their spirits and according to the truths he has revealed in his Word.

With these things in place, we can now consider the final aspect of Jesus' dealing with her.

Jesus revealed himself to her (vv. 25-26)

After Jesus blunted her mention of the controversy on worship, the woman essentially said, 'All of these things are just too difficult for us. We will have to wait until the Messiah comes to sort it all out.' Little did she realize that it was not necessary for her to wait. Jesus identified himself to her in these simple words: 'I who speak to you am He' (v. 26).

The Messiah was nearer than she had realized. He is still near today! He is very near to all who realize their sinful condition. All they must do is cry out to him for cleansing, and they will find it even as the Samaritan woman did.

Gordon J. Keddie writes:

> Christ was nearer than she had known! This remains true in the experience of those who come to him in faith today. Believing in him is always a surprising discovery of free grace, unmerited, undeserved and unsought.[3]

PAUSE TO REFLECT

The Samaritan woman attempted to stop Jesus from zeroing in on her sin by raising a controversial issue. This is still a favourite tactic among unbelievers. Where did Cain get his wife? What about the hypocrites in the church? How can a good God allow evil? Anything to get out of the glare of God's strobe light!

But the woman's ploy did not work. The truth about Jesus was too great to ignore. We would do well to learn from her to not let the things we do not understand obscure the things that we do understand. There will always be things that we cannot explain, but the evidence for Jesus is such that we need not be in doubt about him.

10.

Lessons from a troubled man

◇◇

John 4:46-54

Jesus did many miracles during his public ministry, but the apostle John focuses on only seven in his Gospel. These seven had evidently riveted themselves in his mind in a special way.

The first of these signs was the changing of water into wine at the marriage feast in Cana. The second is reported in the passage before us. Here Jesus heals a young man who was at the point of death (v. 47), and he does it from afar!

This account has much to teach if we only have ears to hear and hearts to obey.

We can and must come to Jesus with our troubles

This royal official had great trouble. His son was critically ill. No parent needs help sympathizing with this man. How parents love their children! How their hearts ache when anything goes wrong with them!

This father did a very wise thing. He went to Jesus. He had heard how Jesus changed water into wine at Cana (v. 46). That miracle was performed in a setting of joy and celebration. Perhaps this same Jesus could be persuaded to perform a miracle in a quite different setting — one of sorrow and gloom.

Archibald Campbell notes: 'Jesus is more than equal to either occasion. He has a place in all circumstances. If we invite Him to our times of innocent happiness, He will increase our joy. If we call on Him in our times of sorrow, anxiety, or bereavement, He can bring consolation, comfort, and a joy that is not of this world.'[1]

Have you learned the lesson this nobleman teaches? Have you learned to go to Jesus with your heartaches and cares?

TIME OUT

What a friend we have in Jesus
All our sins and griefs to bear!
What a privilege it is to carry
Ev'rything to God in prayer!
Oh, what peace we often forfeit,
Oh, what needless pain we bear,
All because we do not carry
Ev'rything to God in prayer!

Have we trials and temptations?
Is there trouble anywhere?
We should never be discouraged,
Take it to the Lord in prayer:
Can we find a friend so faithful
Who will all our sorrows share?
Jesus knows our ev'ry weakness,
Take it to the Lord in prayer

(Joseph Scriven).

The author of those lines got it right — we come to Jesus through prayer.

How this nobleman prayed! His plea was passionate and fervent. He 'implored' Jesus to 'come down and heal his son'.

His prayer was persistent. After Jesus spoke words of rebuke, this man prayed even more fervently: 'Sir, come down before my child dies!' (v. 49).

Many of us come to Jesus with our troubles only to come away feeling that we have not been helped. Could it be that we have come half-heartedly? While we are thinking about this matter of bringing our troubles to Jesus, let us be sure that we understand what our greatest trouble is — our sin and the wrath of God upon it.

The Lord Jesus is sufficient for every trouble, and he is sufficient for this greatest trouble. He did not come to this world primarily to be a healer of men's bodies, but rather to be the healer of their souls. He used the former to picture the latter!

How did he go about this matter of providing healing for the soul? John's Gospel and the other Gospels make the answer abundantly clear. It was by going to the cross to receive the wrath of God against sinners so they never have to experience that wrath themselves.

The nobleman did not realize that his phrase 'my child dies' would have been true even if the son had not been physically ill at the time. His son, as is true of all, was already sick with sin and doomed to die eternally. How many of us tend to think of our children in terms of their physical needs only, and fail to consider their eternal destiny!

J. C. Ryle observes:

He that is wise will never reckon confidently on long life. We never know what a day may bring forth. The strongest and fairest are often cut down and hurried away in a few hours, while the old and feeble linger on for many years.

The only true wisdom is to be always prepared to meet God, to put nothing off which concerns eternity, and to live like men ready to depart at any moment. So living, it matters little whether we die young or old. Joined to the Lord Jesus, we are safe in any event.[2]

We must believe the word of Jesus

After hearing this nobleman pour out his heart, Jesus said, 'Go your way; your son lives' (v. 50). And the apostle John quickly adds: 'So the man believed the word that Jesus spoke to him, and he went his way' (v. 50). Jesus offered no word of explanation and the nobleman asked for none. While this word was sounding in his ears, the Spirit of God was working in his heart to cause him to believe.

This is a picture of saving faith. It is generated in the heart by the Spirit of God using the Word of God (Rom. 10:17). The sword of the Spirit is the Word of God (Eph. 6:17).

J. C. Ryle says:

He that by faith has laid hold on some word of Christ, has got his feet upon a rock. What Christ has said, He is able to do; and what He has undertaken, He will never fail to make good. The sinner who has really reposed his soul on the word of the Lord Jesus, is safe to all eternity. He could not be safer if he saw the Book of Life and his own name written in it.[3]

The word from Jesus brought assurance to the heart of the nobleman. He spoke to Jesus at 1:00 in the afternoon. While there was still time for him to return to Capernaum before dark, he evidently spent the night in Cana because when he met his servants they referred to 'yesterday' when they spoke of his son's recovery (v. 52). He had such assurance about his son that he did not hasten home.

We must believe the truth about Jesus

As the nobleman was making his way home, his servants met him with this happy news: 'Your son lives!' (v. 51).

He immediately asked them the time his son began to improve. Sure enough, it was the very time that Jesus had said, 'Your son lives' (v. 53).

This royal official then knew the truth about Jesus, and he made sure his whole family knew as well. John tells us that the man believed 'and his whole household' (v. 53), which consisted both of his family members and his servants.

The nobleman had pleaded with Jesus to come to the place where his son was. At that point, he didn't understand with whom he was dealing. Now the nobleman and his family knew the truth. Jesus didn't have to come to the place where the child was, and he didn't have to get there before the child died. His power knows no limits.

What did the nobleman and his family believe about Jesus? There can be no doubt about this. John tells us very plainly that he wrote this Gospel so that his readers would believe that Jesus is 'the Christ, the Son of God' (20:31).

And that is exactly what the nobleman and his family believed!

PAUSE TO REFLECT

The question this story puts squarely before us is this: do we believe the truth about Jesus?

The nobleman and his family certainly had plenty of evidence for believing in Jesus, but you and I have even more. The same Jesus who healed the young man went on to heal many others. He also miraculously fed multitudes, stilled storms, cast out demons and raised the dead.

To top it all off, he himself arose from the grave!

There is no need for us to be in suspense about Jesus. The evidence has come in and the verdict has been handed down. Jesus is just exactly what the apostle John claimed him to be — God in human flesh.

It is not enough for us to merely acknowledge this truth. We must think about what this means. Multitudes will give verbal assent to the truth about Jesus. They believe that he was God in human flesh, but they do not allow that truth to change their lives.

If Jesus is God in human flesh, all that he says is true. God cannot lie! And Jesus says that we must believe in him as Lord and Saviour or perish eternally (John 3:14-16; 5:24; 6:40). Furthermore, he says if we have believed in him to the salvation of our souls, we must live in obedience to his commandments (John 14:15,23-24).

Have we taken him as our Lord and Saviour? If so, are we living for him by keeping his commandments?

We do not really believe the truth about Jesus if we do not order our lives according to that truth.

11.

In the grip of truth

◇◇◇

Luke 5:1-11

Simon, James and John had been called by the Lord Jesus Christ to be fishers of men, but they had now abandoned fishing for men in favour of fishing for fish. Perhaps they were still uncertain about Jesus. Or maybe they were uncertain about themselves. It is likely that they were uncertain about both.

These men had undoubtedly assumed that they could go back to their old lives without so much as a single hitch. They could not have been more mistaken.

After a long frustrating night of fishing without success, they had returned to shore and begun cleaning their nets. While they were occupied with that work, Jesus showed up with a huge crowd in tow.

These men had abandoned their responsibility, but Jesus refused to abandon them. Here he is in full pursuit of his reluctant disciples. What delicious irony! The fish the disciples used to catch with ease refused to come anywhere near their nets. But the human fish they had been called to catch were milling all around them and begging to be caught!

The question that had to be answered (vv. 3-5)

These verses indicate that the Lord Jesus put such claims on Simon Peter that he, Peter, had to answer this question: Who is this man?

Jesus first laid claim to one of Simon's possessions by getting into his boat and teaching the people from it. He then put a claim on Simon's time by asking him to get into the boat with him and row out from the shore. This was no small thing. Simon had to be weary, even exhausted, from fishing all night and no doubt was earnestly yearning to find home and bed.

While these claims put Simon to the test, the greatest was yet to come — Jesus staking his claim on Simon's mind by telling him to let down his nets for a catch.

TIME OUT

Net fishing was only done at night, and the disciples had fished all night without catching so much as a single fish. By commanding Simon to let down his nets, Jesus was claiming to know more about fishing than Simon.

This was almost more than Simon could bear. Jesus had been brought up in a carpenter's shop and was now engaged in preaching and teaching. He was no fisherman. Simon, on the other hand, was an expert fisherman.

Imagine the thoughts that went racing through Simon Peter's mind. He may very well have been tempted to speak to Jesus along these lines: 'Now, Jesus, you are a great preacher, and we all appreciate your messages, but you had better leave the fishing to me.'

The real issue before Simon Peter at this point was this: Who was this who was speaking to him? Was he just a carpenter turned preacher, who was intruding into a realm he knew nothing about? Or was he more? The real question was this: What is the truth about this man?

More than two thousand years have come and gone since Simon was forced to ask himself about Jesus of Nazareth. That is a lot of calendar pages in the waste bin! But *the question* has survived them all — Who was Jesus of Nazareth?

To put it another way: Was Jesus a mere man or was he actually God in human flesh? If he was the former, we can safely forget about him, but if he was the latter, we had better think seriously about the implications.

The answer that could not be questioned (vv. 6-7)

The struggle in Simon must have been fierce, but he complied (v. 5). Verses 6 and 7 tell us what happened. Fish that had refused to be caught all night could not wait to get caught! Into the net they went, fish after fish, until the net began to break.

There were so many fish that Simon had to call for James and John to bring their boat out. And even that was not enough. Both boats began to sink. There had never been such a catch of fish!

There was no doubt in Simon's mind about the significance of this catch. Whatever uncertainties the man had been harbouring about Jesus of Nazareth were wiped away as easily as a man removing cobwebs with his hand.

That catch of fish was nothing less than indisputable proof that Jesus was God in human flesh — fully God, fully man, at one and the same time. And he was here demonstrating his authority over his creation.

It hit Simon with sledgehammer force that he was in the presence of God. Simon Peter was in the grip of truth!

While Simon was only a fisherman, his theology was much more sound than many today. He realized that the presence of God is a holy presence, and that he, Simon, sinner that he was, was not fit to be in that presence. So he cried out: 'Depart from me, for I am a sinful man, O Lord!' (v. 8).

The stunning catch of fish gave Simon Peter evidence that he could not ignore. It was indisputable proof that Jesus was indeed God.

The proof that Simon Peter received of Jesus' identity, great as it was, constituted just a small foretaste of the many that were still to come. Jesus did many miracles in the presence of many witnesses, he showed supernatural knowledge of men and their motives and, to cap it all, he arose from the grave.

We need not be in doubt about Jesus. He was fully God and fully man, and, as our living Lord, he continues to be worthy of our love, our obedience and our faithful service.

He is also worthy of our reverence. Let's learn from Simon's response to Jesus (v. 8) to abandon the easy familiarity with God that runs at floodtide these days.

PAUSE TO REFLECT

The Lord Jesus is as much in the claim-making business today as he was in this episode with Simon Peter. He still lays claim to our time and to our possessions, commanding that we show him to be Lord by the ways in which we use these things. Are we heeding these claims? Are we using our time and our possessions to demonstrate his Lordship? Or are we living as if he has no right to claim these things?

The Lord Jesus is also laying claim to our minds, as he did with Simon Peter. He tells us to believe certain things that make no more sense to us than his command to let down the nets made to Simon Peter.

In a society that assures us that men and women are basically good, the Lord tells us that we must believe in the reality and enormity of human sin.

In a world that scoffs at any suggestion of divine judgement, the Lord Jesus tells us to fear him who has the power to cast into hell (Luke 12:5).

It is this same Jesus who tells us that we must believe that the death he died on a Roman cross was no ordinary death. It was not just another man being crucified. In that special death, he received the wrath of God in the place of sinners so that all who repent of their sins and trust him as their Lord and Saviour will never have to endure that wrath themselves.

How the world scoffs at that cross! How quick people are to ridicule it! How could a man dying on a Roman cross outside Jerusalem over 2000 years ago provide eternal salvation? It seems utterly absurd. The apostle Paul got it right: '... the message of the cross is foolishness to those who are perishing...' (1 Cor. 1:18).

The scorn heaped on that cross is so great that many pastors and churches have abandoned the preaching of the cross. If we expect to attract people, we must give them what they want. And they do not want this talk about sin and judgement and a man dying in agony and blood on a cross! So out with it all! And in with clever, witty sermons that tell people how to cope with life's challenges and how to succeed.

When we feel such temptation, we would do well to look at Luke 5 and remember that the Jesus who knew more about fishing than the fisherman also knows more about theology than the theologians. And we would do well to bow in his presence. May God help us all to be in the grip of truth!

12.

Power to forgive

◇◇◇

Mark 2:1-12

There certainly is a lot for us to learn from the four men who carried the paralytic to Jesus. They were obviously men of compassion, faith and ingenuity.

If we will ponder their actions for just a moment, we will have to ask ourselves some probing questions. Are we concerned about those around us? Are we seeking to bring people to the Lord Jesus? Are we willing to take unusual steps to minister, or are we stuck in a rut?

But, having said these things, we must note that this passage is not primarily about these four men and all their commendable qualities. It is about the Lord Jesus Christ. More specifically, it is about the Lord Jesus forgiving this man of his sins (v. 5).

Forgiveness! What a wonderful word! It means our sins have been sent away so they are no longer present. It means a debt has been cancelled so it no longer has to be paid. It means a foul thing has been covered so it can no longer be seen.

If we do not appreciate forgiveness, it is because we do not understand what a terrible thing sin is. Once we see sin in all its ugliness, forgiveness will be the most precious thing in the world.

What can we learn from Jesus forgiving and healing this paralysed man?

The paramount importance of it

Think with me for a moment about the four men of the passage. They had heard that Jesus was in Capernaum, where he had previously preached and performed miracles. Everyone was terribly excited about seeing and hearing Jesus again, and that certainly included these four men.

As they made their way to the house where Jesus was, they decided to bring the paralysed man. Could not the same Jesus who had performed other miracles heal this man? Immediately, they scooped him up and carried him. But when they got to the house they encountered a huge crowd, and no one would allow them to pass.

So they carried the man up to the roof, tore through it and let him down to Jesus.

TIME OUT

◇◇◇◇◇◇◇◇◇◇◇◇◇◇◇◇◇◇◇◇◇◇◇◇◇

Roofs in those days consisted of branches from trees which were covered with mud or clay that was mixed with straw, all of which would have posed no problem for four men to dismantle. Access to the roof may very well have been possible by an outside staircase or by a couple of the men pulling themselves up on the roof where they were handed the ropes by the men remaining on the ground. The other men would then have joined their friends on the roof to pull up the pallet of the paralysed man.

I wonder if you will agree with me that their hope and expectation was that Jesus would heal the man of his paralysis. They were in for a surprise. With the man before him, Jesus said, 'Son, your sins are forgiven you' (v. 5).

What are we to make of this? Isn't it obvious that Jesus regarded this man as having a far greater problem than physical paralysis? Seeing that far greater problem, Jesus addressed it and ignored the paralysis for the moment. Jesus understood something that we have so much difficulty understanding, namely, that this man would have been far better off to have remain paralysed with his sins forgiven than to have been well and not forgiven.

Jesus would later state the importance of forgiveness very pointedly: 'It is better for you to enter into life lame or maimed, rather than having two hands or two feet, to be cast into the everlasting fire' (Matt. 18:8).

How we need to learn from Jesus! Eternal life is more important than anything, and eternal life can be ours only if our sins are forgiven. How parents need to learn this! Our children can enter into heaven without ball games and web sites, but they cannot enter it without forgiveness! Parents, are you teaching your children the vital importance of forgiveness?

The ability or the authority of Jesus to forgive sins

The words of Jesus outraged the religious leaders who were there. They began muttering to themselves: 'Why does this Man speak blasphemies like this? Who can forgive sins but God alone?' (v. 7).

They were right. God and God alone can forgive sins. And if Jesus had not been God, they would have been correct that Jesus had no right to grant forgiveness. Jesus would have been a blasphemer if he had not been God!

It never occurred to these men that Jesus could be God in human flesh and, therefore, have the authority to forgive sins. So Jesus determined that he would give them unimpeachable evidence that he was the God-man.

He did so in two ways. First, he told them what they were thinking (v. 8). Secondly, he healed the man.

He prefaced that healing by asking the religious leaders this question: 'Which is easier, to say to the paralytic, "Your sins are forgiven you," or to say, "Arise, take up your bed and walk"?' (v. 9).

As he turned to the paralytic he said, 'But that you may know that the Son of Man has power on earth to forgive sins, I say to you, arise, take up your bed, and go to your house' (vv. 10-11).

Immediately, the man sprang from his bed (v. 12).

So Jesus healed the man physically in order to show that he had the power and authority to heal spiritually. He healed him of his paralysis to show he had the authority to grant forgiveness. If his word of healing had been effective, how could anyone doubt that his word of forgiveness had been?

The proper response to it (v. 12)

There were certainly plenty of witnesses to the healing of this paralysed man. There was a large crowd there to hear Jesus, and they all saw this man who was carried to the roof on his bed carrying that very bed as he walked out. And Mark tells us that all were 'amazed' and all 'glorified God, saying, "We never saw anything like this!"' (v. 12).

They had not seen anything like this before because they had never seen anyone like Jesus before! God was now among men! The eternal one had come into this temporal realm! The Creator was among his creatures! The mighty God was demonstrating his authority! The caring God was demonstrating his grace!

They marvelled at the miracle of physical healing, but, as we have noted, that was the lesser miracle. The greater was the forgiveness of the man's sins. All God's people have received that miracle. Let us make sure that we are living in such a way that we demonstrate the greatness of it. Let's make sure we are living in such a way that we are glorifying the God of grace who stoops to unworthy sinners and forgives them.

PAUSE TO REFLECT

The same Lord Jesus has spoken words of forgiveness to all of us, if we care to believe them. He has promised that he will forgive the sins of all those who come to him in true repentance and faith. But Satan is always busy assuring us that those words are not true. So the question arises: How do we know that Jesus can and will forgive our sins?

The answer is that he has given us sufficient evidence even as he gave to the religious leaders on that distant occasion. This evidence is presented in the Bible. Jesus performed all kinds of miracles in front of all kinds of witnesses. He even raised three people from the dead! To cap it all off, he himself arose from the dead. It is important once again to remember that there were many witnesses of all that Jesus did.

The evidence for Jesus is so convincing and compelling that we need not be in doubt about him. He was God in flesh. And if he was God, his words are true. God cannot lie. If he has promised to forgive our sins, we have absolutely no reason to question it. Forgiveness is ours, if we will only claim it! Let's claim it, saying with the psalmist:

If you, Lord, should mark iniquities,
O Lord, who could stand?
But there is forgiveness with You...

(Ps. 130:3-4).

So far as we know, the religious leaders refused to believe the evidence that Jesus gave them. Will you believe the evidence that Jesus has given you? Or will you repeat their error?

13.

The mysterious and the plain

◇◇◇

John 5:1-9

This passage brings us to the third sign of John's Gospel. Here Jesus heals a man who had been lame for thirty-eight years. This healing took place in Jerusalem where Jesus had gone to attend an unnamed feast (v. 1).

This passage also intertwines things that are mysterious with things that are exceedingly plain and clear.

The mysterious

We are first faced with the mystery of human suffering. Here is a man who had been lame for thirty-eight long years. That was a longer time than most people lived in those days.

We are familiar with the mystery of human suffering. We see it all around us all the time. Terrorists strike, and people die. Sickness strikes, and people die. Millions are put to death each year while they are still in their mothers' wombs!

All suffer in this life in some form or fashion, but some suffer to a far greater degree than others, and we are left scratching our heads and wondering why.

What causes all the pain and suffering in this world? The Bible tells us that the world is not as God made it. When God created there was no sickness or death. These things came in as a result of sin. We should not allow, therefore, the calamities of life to make us angry at God. We should rather be angry at sin.

TIME OUT

J. C. Ryle notes:

> When we read of cases of sickness like this, we should remember how deeply we ought to hate sin! Sin was the original root, and cause, and fountain of every disease in the world. God did not create man to be full of aches, and pains, and infirmities. These things are the fruits of the Fall. There would have been no sickness, if there had been no sin.[1]

But having said that sin is the reason for suffering, we still wonder why some suffer more than others and why good people often suffer far more than those that are not good. It is a mystery!

This passage also brings before us the mystery of the pool. Here we have a great multitude of sick people in Jerusalem at the pool of Bethesda (house of outpouring). This pool, located inside the Sheep Gate of the city, was circled by five 'porches'. These were covered colonnades.

The reason for this large gathering was the belief that an angel would come and stir the pool, and the first person who stepped in after the stirring would be healed of his affliction (v. 4).

The fact that the oldest manuscripts of John's Gospel do not contain the last part of verse 3 and all of verse 4 has caused many to conclude that we are dealing with superstition here rather than with an actual appearance of an angel. Others argue that we should take the passage as it stands.

There is little agreement on this pool. It is another mystery!

The plain

I have often said that we should never allow the things that we do not understand to obscure the things that we do understand. We have mysteries in this passage for sure, but, happily, there is something here that is as clear as the noonday sun, and that is the truth about the Lord Jesus Christ. How very easy it is for us to get so wrapped up in the mysteries that we fail to see the truth!

Now what is the truth about Jesus? It is the same truth that we have been encountering throughout this series: Jesus was no ordinary man. How are we to explain him? He was God in human flesh! The God-man!

That is quite an assertion. What is the evidence for it?

The perfect knowledge of Jesus

As Jesus passed by the pool, he came upon this man. There is no indication that he, the lame man, had any knowledge of Jesus or what Jesus had done. But Jesus had knowledge of him (v. 6). He knew he would be there at the pool, and he knew how very long he had been lame.

The abounding grace of Jesus

Jesus singled him out of the multitude of sick people and asked if he wanted to be well. This question was necessary because many of the sick and lame of that day made a fairly lucrative living through begging and did not really want to give it up.

How marvellous is the grace that Jesus manifested to this poor man! This act of grace compelled S. G. DeGraaf to say:

> Contrary to the Bethesda spring, God's grace is not a spring that flows only intermittently; it is a spring that supplies water constantly. Such grace heals us completely and for ever.[2]

The wonderful power of Jesus

This passage not only reveals the power of Jesus, but also puts the power of Jesus on display.

When the man indicated that he did want to be well (v. 7), Jesus simply said, 'Rise, take up your bed and walk' (v. 8). John notes that the man was 'immediately' on his feet and walking (v. 9).

This was none other than the power of God!

PAUSE TO REFLECT

But what does this passage have to do with us? Why are we even taking the time to consider it? The answer is that the same things that were true of Jesus in this passage are still true.

Are you face to face with the mystery of human suffering? The Lord Jesus knows all about you. Your suffering is not hidden from his eyes. He knows you with a perfect knowledge, and he also knows the purpose behind your suffering. Yes, there is a purpose behind it all. Nothing comes to the people of God that has not passed through the hands of their loving heavenly Father, and all that passes through his hands to them is for their good and for his glory (Rom. 8:28).

The mysterious and the plain

We want very much for God to explain the purpose now, but the Lord wants us to trust him now. The explanation will come later.

Trials dark on every hand,
And we cannot understand
All the ways that God would lead us
To that blessed promised land;
But He'll guide us with His eye,
And we'll follow till we die;
We will understand it better by and by

(Charles A. Tindley).

The same Jesus also abounds in grace towards his people even as he did with this lame man. He not only knows about us with a perfect knowledge, he also cares for us with a perfect care.

His caring heart does not mean that he always delivers us from our suffering, but we can be sure that he will always be present to strengthen, help and comfort us.

And the powerful Jesus of John 5 is powerful today. But what good is that power if he does not use it to deliver his people from their hardships and difficulties? When the Lord does not deliver, it is, as we have noted, because he has a beneficial purpose in mind. But the fact that he possesses that power guarantees that he will eventually deliver us from all suffering and bring us into the glory of his presence (2 Tim. 4:18).

This passage also conveys a powerful message to those who have not received the Lord Jesus as their Saviour.

We all come into this world spiritually lamed. We are unable to achieve God's purpose for our lives unless something is done to make us spiritually whole.

The good news is that the same Lord Jesus Christ who healed this man provides spiritual healing. He forgives sinners of their sins and grants them the promise of eternal life.

Let us be clear about the basis on which Jesus does these things. It is only through his death on the cross. On that cross, he actually received the wrath of God in the place of sinners so that all who repent of their sins and trust completely in him will never have to receive that wrath themselves.

Are you conscious of your sins? Are you aware that you stand guilty before a holy God? There is a Saviour. His name is Jesus. He knows you, and he has grace and power sufficient for you to be saved from your sins. Run to him today.

14.

A doubting saint

◇◇◇◇◇◇◇◇◇◇◇◇◇◇◇◇◇◇◇◇◇◇◇◇◇◇◇◇◇◇◇◇◇◇◇◇◇

Matthew 11:2-12

This passage brings us to a very remarkable thing. Here we have that robust saint of God, John the Baptist, in the clutches of doubt.

This is the man that had boldly pointed to Jesus and cried: 'Behold! The Lamb of God who takes away the sin of the world!' (John 1:29).

But now John the Baptist is in prison, and the faith that once soared like the eagle has hit the ground. From his prison cell, John sends messengers to Jesus to ask: 'Are You the Coming One, or do we look for another?' (v. 3).

Such a man asking such a question!

Difficulties can certainly clip the wings of faith. Perhaps that is what has happened here. Perhaps prison has taken its toll.

Or it could be that we are to find the reason for John's lapse in the type of ministry that Jesus was exercising. John's ministry had been of a fiery nature — denouncing sin, promising wrath and calling for repentance.

But the ministry of Jesus had a gentleness about it. Needs were being met, sins were being forgiven and broken hearts were being mended.

Or it could be that John was holding the common messianic view of his day, believing that the Messiah would defeat Israel's enemies and set up an earthly kingdom.

Whatever the reason, the doubt was real. We all know about doubt. There are thousands of things that can feed it. Christ's kingdom seems to be advancing so slowly, evil seems to be progressing so rapidly, and his followers seem to follow so poorly. Disdain and contempt for the Christian message seem to be growing by leaps and bounds. And the church is hampered in her mission by pettiness, selfishness, stubbornness and childishness! How much of the church's life is driven by leaders trying to make sure that people do not 'get their feelings hurt'! How much time the church spends with her hands tied because her members are tied to the past and unwilling to make necessary changes!

Then there is our individual performance as Christians. We claim to be in touch with the power of God through Jesus, but we find ourselves giving in to various sins, and we find it difficult to do even the most elementary duties.

Perhaps the Baptist was right! Maybe the problem is that there is nothing to our Christianity after all. Maybe we have been mistaken to fasten our faith and pin our hopes on Jesus, and now we just need the courage to admit the truth. Maybe it is time to consign Christianity to history's graveyard of failed movements. Maybe it is time to look for something else!

Fairness demands that we do not turn away before we give Jesus the opportunity to answer. He answered John, and his answer deserves our consideration, as does what Jesus said about John.

What Jesus said to John (vv. 4-6)

How did Jesus respond when the messengers from John arrived with their question? It is interesting that he offered no rebuke of John. He rather told the messengers to tell John what they themselves had seen and heard while they had been there with him, Jesus.

What had they seen? People who had been blind were now seeing. People who had been lame were now walking. Lepers were now clean. Deaf people were now hearing, and dead people were now living.

And what had they, the messengers from John, heard while they were there with Jesus? They had heard the gospel preached!

Jesus did not tell them why John was suffering in prison. He did not tell them why he was not conducting the kind of ministry that John expected. Those questions were left unanswered as Jesus pointed them to answers that could not be questioned.

What did the things that Jesus was doing say about him? Ordinary men do not cause the blind to see, the lame to walk and the deaf to hear. They do not cleanse lepers. And they certainly do not raise the dead.

These deeds powerfully declared that there was only one explanation for Jesus. He was indeed the very person that John had proclaimed him to be. He was God in human flesh, and he was here to take away sin.

In saying these things, Jesus gave a further proof of his messiahship. We can be sure that John's messengers knew the Old Testament, and as they listened to Jesus they realized that he was quoting from the prophet Isaiah (Isa. 29:18; 35:4-6; 61:1). These were the true marks of the Messiah, not the setting up of an earthly kingdom as John may have expected. Jesus was claiming that he was fulfilling Scripture.

The things to which Jesus pointed John were undisputed facts, and Jesus was calling John to not let his questions crowd out the facts. He was not to let what he did not understand obscure what he did understand.

The same message applies to us. Why do so many hardships come our way? Why does evil flourish? Why does God not do more to advance his kingdom?

We do not know. But we know that Jesus was no ordinary man. We know that he did indeed do the miracles he mentioned, that he fulfilled prophecy after prophecy and that he capped it all off with his own resurrection from the dead. All of these things tell us that he was God in human flesh, and, as God, he is worthy of our faith and our devotion. We can, therefore, hold the questions that are not answered as we rejoice in the questions that have been decisively and indisputably answered.

Jesus had yet one more thing to say to those messengers from John: 'And blessed is he who is not offended because of Me' (v. 6).

What was Jesus saying? He was telling John the Baptist that there was a choice before him. He could accept Jesus as the Christ that he was, or he could stumble over him. But he could not change him into the Christ that he, John the Baptist, wanted. Blessing comes to those who accept Christ as he is!

What Jesus said about John (vv. 7-11)

When John's messengers left, Jesus turned to the multitude, who presumably had heard his conversation with the messengers.

The things he says to these people about John the Baptist are stunningly wonderful. These people had heard the messengers of John express his doubts to Jesus. Now these messengers have departed, and Jesus is left with the crowd. They are obviously wondering about John the Baptist. What does Jesus have to say to them? It is very interesting. He does not call John a failure, a turncoat or a traitor.

Rather, he commends him in the strongest possible terms. John was not a reed shaken in the wind (v. 7). More than a prophet, he was the forerunner of Christ (vv. 9-10). As such, he occupied a special place in God's plan, a place that gave John a greatness that no one else could rival (v. 11).

What we have in the words of Jesus is something that is comforting beyond measure. While others saw doubt and weakness in John, the Lord Jesus saw faith and strength.

TIME OUT

The devil is ever eager to point to our doubts and cause us to conclude that we have little faith, but the Lord would have us know that little faith is still faith. While the devil magnifies the doubt, the Lord magnifies the faith.

Because of their sins, the people of Judah saw their beautiful Jerusalem destroyed, and they themselves were carried into captivity in Babylon. There in Babylon, they carried the mental picture of the ruins of Jerusalem. But the Lord spoke to them there and said, 'Your walls are continually before Me' (Isa. 49:16). Where they saw ruins, God saw walls!

That's the way it is with God. When we can see nothing but our doubts, he sees our faith, and when it seems to us that our faith will fail, he knows that it will not. You see, faith is his gift. He is the author and finisher of it (Heb. 12:2), and he will not allow it to die.

PAUSE TO REFLECT

Having commended John the Baptist, the Lord Jesus strongly urged the multitude to get into his, Jesus', kingdom (v. 12). In other words, they were not to allow John's doubt to cause them to miss the important thing — getting into the kingdom (v. 12). How many people are doing this! Because they see the failings of Christians, they stay out of the kingdom themselves! Where is the wisdom in that?

When you are in the dark, hang on to that which you saw in the light.

Jesus was telling John that blessing comes to those who do not allow their questions and confusion to drive them away from him. Those who persist in trusting even when they don't understand will find true blessing at last.

15.

Great gratitude for great mercy

◇◇◇

Luke 7:36-50

We have here a gripping episode. Simon the Pharisee had invited Jesus to dine at his home. We should not take this to mean that Simon had any real affection or admiration for Jesus. Quite the contrary! His lack of affection is clearly proven by his failure to perform the most basic functions of a host. He had not washed Jesus' feet (v. 44), greeted him with the customary kiss (v. 45), or anointed his head with oil (v. 46).

The Pharisees hated Jesus and enjoyed setting traps for him. This supper was designed to give Simon the opportunity to closely observe Jesus and to confirm Simon's dislike for him.

In that time houses were quite different from ours. There was an openness about them that allowed people who were passing by to merely walk in without knocking or being announced.

A woman, whom we presume was widely known as immoral, took advantage of the openness and walked in. She was a woman on a mission. She had heard that Jesus was there, and she went straight to him. She planned to anoint him with the ointment she had brought, but she was so overwhelmed at the sight of him that she began weeping, her tears falling on his feet. And then, embarrassed at the sight of her tears on his feet, and having nothing to dry with, she loosed the long tresses of her hair and began drying his feet.

Simon didn't have a clue. As far as he was concerned, he had achieved his purpose in inviting Jesus to his home. Jesus couldn't possibly be a prophet, or he would have known what a sinful woman this was and would never have allowed her to touch him! Simon was ready to pronounce Jesus a fraud. But Jesus cut through his musings with a parable that perfectly read the inner workings of his mind. The parable had to do with two men in debt to their master. One owed five hundred denarii, the other fifty. Neither man had anything to pay with, but the master 'freely forgave them both' (v. 42).

There is so much here for us to learn and appreciate!

Jesus can and does forgive sins!

He can forgive sins because he is no mere man. He is God! God in human flesh!

And he does forgive sins! This woman found it to be true. Although deeply stained by sin, she was forgiven by Jesus. If you think that you are too great a sinner to be saved, you are completely wrong! The grace of God is greater than all our sins.

Jesus made this clear in his parable. Here was a man who owed fifty denarii, and over here was a man who owed five hundred. Neither man could pay. Did the creditor say, 'I can forgive the smaller amount, but not the larger'?

No, not at all! Jesus said, '...he freely forgave them both' (v. 42).

What good news this is! Jesus can forgive those who, although outwardly moral and respectable, are still sinners. But he can also forgive those who have plumbed the depths of wickedness. No sinner is too sinful to be saved.

Consciousness of forgiveness is the root of deep devotion to the Lord

No one will quarrel about this — the woman in this passage felt deep love for the Lord Jesus. She risked ridicule and scorn in order to show that love.

How did she come to have such love? It sprang from the realization that she, a great sinner, had received great mercy.

TIME OUT

We must be careful that we do not 'put the cart before the horse.' She showed love to Jesus because she had already been forgiven — and not in order to receive forgiveness. J. C. Ryle rightly says, 'Her love was the effect of her forgiveness, not the cause, — the consequence of her forgiveness, not the condition, — the result of her forgiveness, not the reason, — the fruit of her forgiveness, not the root.'[1]

Ryle further writes: 'We must work from life, and not for life.'[2]

But why did Jesus say to her, 'Your sins are forgiven' (v. 48), if her sins had previously been forgiven? Ryle says this was 'a public and authoritative declaration' of the forgiveness she had received.[3]

William Hendriksen offers this explanation: 'What the woman already knew in principle is now reaffirmed. In view of her past life in sin she probably needed this reassurance, so that what she already sensed to be true ... might become even more firmly established in her heart, namely, that once for all and completely her sins had been and were now blotted out.'[4]

Having been forgiven, this woman could not do enough to show her love for Jesus.

Matthew Henry writes:

> The greater sinners any have been before their conversion, the greater saints they should be after... When a persecuting Saul became a preaching Paul he laboured more abundantly.[5]

Have you ever noticed how some people just cannot seem to do enough for Christ? They are anxious to take up any task that will advance the kingdom of Christ and they do so without so much as a whimper of self-pity.

Then there are those who appear to find it difficult, if not impossible, to do the smallest thing for Christ. Even though they profess to believe in Christ as their Saviour, they find serving him to be a drudgery.

How are we to explain the difference between these two groups? Both profess to know Christ. But to one group Christ is apparently everything, while to the other he is scarcely anything. How is it that the same Christ can at one and the same time inspire such devotion and such indifference? This passage lays a clear sequence before us: (1) we won't serve Christ if we don't love him; (2) we won't love Christ if we don't know forgiveness; (3) we won't know forgiveness if we don't know our sinfulness.

Lack of love for Christ means lack of forgiveness

What about that 'human iceberg' sitting there at the table with Jesus while this woman was expressing her love? What about Simon? He had not provided for the washing of Jesus' feet. He had not kissed him. Nor had he anointed him. He had done nothing that the woman had done (vv. 44-46).

There is no difficulty here. The reason Simon had not done these things is that he didn't love Christ. And the reason he did not love Christ is because he had not been forgiven. While Jesus plainly said to the woman that her sins were forgiven (v. 48), he said no such thing to Simon.

Why is it, then, that Simon had not been forgiven? Was it because Christ was unwilling or unable to forgive him? No! Christ was just as willing and able to forgive Simon as he had been with the woman. The difference was that the woman realized her sinfulness, but Simon did not realize his.

It seems that at the end of this parable Jesus was saying to Simon, 'I have already forgiven this woman who owed five hundred pence and I can forgive your fifty pence. Would you like to be forgiven?'

But Simon was apparently unwilling to recognize that he was just as much in need of forgiveness as the woman. Simon's whole problem was in thinking his state before God was radically different from the woman's when, in fact, it was exactly the same. The fact that he had not lived a life of sinful degradation didn't change another fact — he was still a sinner and was just as helpless to pay his debt to God as this woman who had plumbed the depths of sin!

So he never knew the forgiveness the woman knew, and he never felt the love for Christ the woman felt.

Nothing is harder than convincing people of their sinfulness. Many who profess to be saved show little love for Christ because they fancy that their sins were not very bad, therefore they don't owe Christ very much. Nothing could be farther from the truth. Those who are truly saved owe Christ all the love they can muster because they were all sinners and all equally unable to pay.

PAUSE TO REFLECT

In his sermon on this passage, Alexander Maclaren asks this question: 'Why is it that such multitudes of you professing Christians are such icebergs in your Christianity?'[6]

Then he answers his question by saying: 'Mainly for this reason — that you have never found out in anything like an adequate measure, how great a sinner you are, and how sure and sweet and sufficient Christ's pardoning mercy is.'[7]

16.

A man hopelessly possessed

Mark 5:1-20

The fifth chapter of Mark's Gospel is devoted to hopeless people finding hope through the power and grace of the Lord Jesus Christ.

A hopelessly possessed man is freed from his demons (vv. 1-20). A hopelessly ill woman is made well (vv. 25-34). And a hopelessly bereaved father is lifted from the pit of despair (vv. 21-24, 35-43).

What a cheering chapter this is! How we need its message of hope! The same Lord Jesus who gave hope on these occasions is alive and well and still giving hope to hopeless people!

Few cases could be more hopeless than the demon-possessed man presented in the above passage. Let's consider these verses under three headings.

The Satanic domination

No sooner had Jesus and his disciples set foot in the country of the Gerasenes than they were met with this fierce, violent man who was completely dominated by Satan.

TIME OUT

Many scoff at the mere mention of demon possession. They argue that this was the only way the poor, simple folk of that day could explain illness.

It seems to escape the notice of these people that the Bible always distinguishes between illness and demon possession (Matt. 4:24). When a person was sick, the Bible names his ailment, and when one was demon-possessed Scripture explicitly says so.

Demon possession was especially prevalent during Jesus' ministry. It seems the work of Jesus provoked Satan to go on a rampage. And as history winds down, we can expect Satan to go on one final fling. We are even now seeing more and more instances of demon possession.

This story alone ought to remove all doubts about the possibility of demon possession. Alexander Maclaren observes: 'The awful picture of this demoniac is either painted from life, or it is one of the most wonderful feats of poetic imagination. Nothing more terrible, vivid, penetrating and real was ever conceived by the greatest creative genius.'[1]

Please note the characteristics of this satanically dominated man.

His astounding power (vv. 3-4)

Evidently, the citizens of the community had at one time been able to bind him; but as his condition progressively worsened, his strength increased.

By the time Jesus confronted him he was well past binding. He was able to snap chains as though they were twigs. And the inhabitants of the area had simply ceased trying to control him, being content to avoid the area completely and leave him to himself.

His pain (v. 5)

He was in great mental anguish for he was constantly crying out day and night. And this led him to inflict severe physical pain upon himself. Mark says he constantly gashed himself with stones.

His personality (vv. 6-10)

He obviously had multiple personalities. The demons had so taken control of him that he was unable to speak. The demons spoke through him. When Jesus asked for his name, one demon spoke for all: 'My name is Legion; for we are many' (v. 9).

It is interesting to observe the interplay here between the singular and the plural pronouns. Verse 10 says, 'Also he begged Him earnestly that He would not send them out of the country.'

This is typical of demon possession. The demons take control of the personality and speak and work through it.

It is also noteworthy that the demons who possessed this man instinctively knew Jesus. That's why the man was compelled to bow down before him and to confess that Jesus was the 'Son of the Most High God' (vv. 6-7).

There was never any question that Jesus had the power to do with these demons whatever he wished. They acknowledged this throughout the entire episode.

The majestic demonstration of Jesus' power (vv. 11-13)

Knowing that Jesus could do with them as he wished, the demons pleaded with him to allow them to go into a nearby herd of swine.

They desperately wanted to stay in that country (v. 10). Why was this important to them? Some think they merely felt more comfortable in an area of tombs, skeletons and desolation. Others speculate that demons were assigned to certain areas. If Jesus were to cast them out of their area, they would have to enter hell itself (see Luke 8:31).

Whatever the reason for their desire, Jesus granted it. This also raises questions. Why did the demons want to go into the pigs? They always desire to possess something, and they obviously knew Jesus would not allow them to possess another human being. So the pigs were the next best choice. This would indicate that the demons did not know that the pigs would react by plunging into the sea.

But why did Jesus allow them to go into the pigs? He knew what would happen. Why did he allow the destruction of these pigs and the loss it caused their owners?

By allowing the demons to possess the swine, Jesus gave visible, powerful and indisputable proof of two things: the destructive power of Satan and the greater power of Jesus.

We have here a parable in action. Allowing the demons to enter the swine placed spiritual realities in bold relief. On one hand, there was Satan with his desire to destroy and ruin. On the other hand, there was Jesus with his compassion and his power over Satan.

The issue could not have been more clear cut. In Satan there is only misery, wretchedness and destruction. In Jesus Christ there is hope and life. The Lord Jesus is the Creator and Sustainer of all, and his decision to destroy part of the physical creation in order to drive home spiritual truths is part of his lordship.

It has been necessary throughout history for God to shatter men's material possessions in order to wake them up to spiritual things. We should be very careful about criticizing God about any course he pursues. Our wisdom is nothing compared to his (Isa. 55:8-9; Rom. 11:33-36).

The tragic decision of the citizens (vv. 14-20)

After the pigs drowned, the herders immediately ran to the city to tell what had happened. The people came out and found Jesus and the man, who was now calm and clothed (v. 15).

But their minds were not on the miraculous change in this man. That appears to have been the farthest thing from their minds! Mark says they were frightened! (v. 15).

Isn't this amazing? We could certainly understand them being frightened when this man was dominated by Satan and posed a threat to the community. But why were they frightened by a man who was obviously no threat?

The truth is that they were not afraid of the man at all. They were afraid of Jesus! Dr Martyn Lloyd-Jones explains their fear. He says these citizens had '...a feeling that He who had done so much to this demoniac and also to the swine, not only had sufficient power to do the same to them, but probably would insist upon doing so'.[2]

Lloyd-Jones further writes of Jesus:

He seemed to be able to do anything He liked and no one could stop Him. It has been suggested that the loss of the swine accounted for this feeling. It may have done so up to a point, but there was still a greater loss. He would change their entire lives, He would rule and govern them. That would mean an end to everything they liked and enjoyed. All their sins would have to go.[3]

In light of this new 'threat', they asked Jesus to depart. He had amply demonstrated that there was hope in him for power over Satan and over sin, but they determined to reject the hope.

PAUSE TO REFLECT

Isn't it amazing what we are willing to live with? We will live with the wretchedness, the misery, the ruined and shattered lives that Satan and sin create, all because we do not want our lives changed by Jesus Christ! Ultimately, the question of our day is not whether there is any hope. Jesus Christ has answered that clearly in his death and resurrection. Ultimately, the question is whether we will accept the hope Jesus Christ offers.

17.

A woman hopelessly ill

Mark 5:25-34

This passage really tells us about a miracle within a miracle. Jesus was on his way to heal Jairus' daughter when he was interrupted by a touch on his garment.

How pitiful was this woman! She had suffered from a haemorrhage for twelve long years. Her suffering certainly wasn't due to any unwillingness to seek help. She had consulted several doctors, but not one was able to help her. In fact, her condition grew progressively worse under their care.

She really had reached the end of her tether for she didn't have any money left to experiment with any more 'cures'. For all practical purposes her case was hopeless. Just as Legion appeared to be hopelessly possessed by Satan (vv. 1-20), so this woman appeared to be hopelessly sick.

Perhaps the woman had resigned herself to her fate when a glimmer of hope broke through her dark sky. She heard about Jesus and his mighty power — power great enough to handle hopeless cases like hers. On hearing these glorious tidings, she resolved to go and touch him. If she could just do that, all would be well!

Had we been there we could have told her how misinformed she was. She obviously had faith all mixed up with superstition. She seemed to think Christ was some sort of magician, who exuded power to those who touched him.

Yes, there was superstition here, but there was also real faith. It's possible for faith to be flawed and still be genuine. We sometimes create the impression that a person's theology has to be 100% sound before he can be saved. I certainly am an advocate of soundness in theology, but I'm also grateful that Christ does not require that we have a seminary diploma before we can be saved! Let this woman come and touch Christ. He will release his power to her flawed faith so she can be healed and brought to more perfect faith.

With these things in mind, let's see what further lessons this woman can teach us.

We can touch Christ and yet not really touch him (vv. 25-28)

A great crowd was around Jesus when Jairus came and pleaded with him to come and heal his daughter. As Jesus and Jairus set off together, the curious, thrill-seeking throng accompanied them. The crush must have been terrific when they entered the narrow streets of the city, and Jesus was repeatedly bumped and jostled by the crowd.

All of this was to the sick woman's advantage. Her plan was simply to touch Jesus and then melt silently into the crowd. She was very anxious to remain undetected because her disease caused her to be ceremonially unclean, along with any who came into contact with her. She assumed Jesus would not knowingly want to touch her or be touched by her.

She also wanted to be spared the embarrassment of revealing the condition for which she sought a cure. So slowly and steadily we can see her making her way through the mass of humanity until she is able to reach out and touch Jesus.

Although Jesus was being constantly bumped and jostled, he recognized that touch. It was different from all the others. The other contact was accidental, from those who were merely curious. This touch was intentional, from one who was earnestly serious. Jesus felt that touch and he responded to it.

Others in that crowd had needs Jesus could have met, but no one else reached out to him in faith. Dean Trench writes of the woman:

> She came expecting a blessing, believing a blessing, and so finding the blessing which she expected and believed... But that careless multitude who thronged the Lord, only eager to gratify their curiosity, and to see what new wonder he would next do, as they desired nothing, expected nothing from him, so they obtained nothing. Empty they came, and empty they went away.[1]

There are still two types of contact with Christ today. Some come into contact with him carelessly and out of curiosity. They come to church, sit in the pews, sing the songs and hear Christ presented; but they never seek to bring their needs to him. They feel it's enough for them just to be part of the throng. It's not that they have no need for Christ. They do! It's not that Christ cannot help them. He can! It's rather that they refuse to bring their need to Christ.

It is when we reach out to him as this woman did, conscious of our great need and confident of his mighty power, that we discover that Christ can indeed help us.

We cannot truly touch Christ without being changed (vv. 29-30)

As soon as she touched Christ, she was conscious of complete, instantaneous healing. We can only stand in awe of such power. It certainly is a far cry from many of the so-called 'healings' today, which are neither instantaneous nor complete.

Let's be careful we don't lose sight of the fact that this power resided in the person of Jesus Christ. It is easy for us to do so with this particular incident. Some religions make much of certain relics, things that Jesus was supposed to have touched or used, as though power resided in those relics. But the fact that Jesus' power was released to this woman through her touch of his garment should not obscure the fact that the power resided in Christ, not in his garment.

He chose to heal this woman in this way, but he was not laying down a precedent for us to seek his power through mere external things. William L. Lane writes:

> The healing of the woman occurred through God's free and gracious decision to bestow upon her the power which was active in Jesus. By an act of sovereign will God determined to honor the woman's faith in spite of the fact that it was tinged with ideas which bordered on magic.[2]

That same power still resides in Christ, and the primary manifestation of his power is in saving those who repent and believe. Paul calls the gospel of Christ 'the power of God to salvation for everyone who believes' (Rom. 1:16).

The sinner's condition is much like this woman's. Sin is incurable as far as human agencies or remedies are concerned. What is the sinner to do?

Let him reach out in faith to Christ! There he will find power to forgive and cleanse him of his sins. The power of Christ's salvation is so great that Paul writes: 'Therefore, if anyone is in Christ, he is a new creation; old things have passed away; behold, all things have become new' (2 Cor. 5:17).

Let us now consider another lesson we can learn from this woman.

Coming to Jesus means coming out of the crowd (vv. 30-34)

As soon as Jesus felt power released to heal this woman, he turned and began looking for her. His question, 'Who touched Me?' seemed to be ridiculous to the disciples (v. 31). But Jesus ignored their rudeness and continued looking for the woman.

The woman finally came forward on her own. Evidently concluding that she could not escape detection, the woman decided to admit what she had done.

TIME OUT

We can readily understand why she was 'fearing and trembling' (v. 33).

William Hendriksen says:

At that time and in that country for a woman to speak in public was generally considered improper. This all the more on a subject such as this, the particular physical scourge by which she had been afflicted. And would not even the fact that she, in that condition, deliberately had touched the Master add to the impropriety in the eyes of the bystanders? Yes, and even, perhaps, in the eyes of Jesus Himself? Would he scold her perhaps?[3]

Her fears were unfounded. Jesus didn't call her forward to scold her but rather to make sure that she did not go away with a mistaken notion about her healing. It was not because of the physical touch but rather because of the faith behind that touch.

By calling her out of the crowd, Jesus also gave her the opportunity to proclaim God's grace and power. Her testimony was necessary to glorify God, to benefit others, and to strengthen and confirm her own faith.

PAUSE TO REFLECT

Many are like this woman. They want Christ to meet their needs and then sneak away, clutching the blessings, while remaining anonymous. Christ has shown us through this woman that he won't allow us to get away with that. If we have been transformed by him, we can never be the same again. We must now live for him. Knowing Christ always means coming out of the crowd. Have you been called out of the crowd to live for him?

18.
A father hopelessly bereaved

Mark 5:21-24,35-43

So far we have found Jesus delivering a man who appeared to be hopelessly possessed, and healing a woman who appeared to be hopelessly sick. Now this chapter builds to a giant, swelling crescendo with Jesus triumphing over an even more hopeless case — one in which death had occurred. Truly, he is the hope of the hopeless!

This particular incident began with hope, but it quickly degenerated into deep, dark despair. When Jairus set out to find Jesus, his daughter was desperately ill, but still alive. That was cause for at least a faint glimmer of hope. And Jesus had agreed to accompany Jairus to his home — a bright ray of hope!

But as Jairus observed the slow progress of Jesus through the enormous crowd, doubt began to set in. Then, to make matters worse, a woman interrupted Jesus.

Jairus must have been heartened by this amazing demonstration of Jesus' healing power upon the woman, but he also must have felt all hope for his daughter melting down and oozing silently away.

Then suddenly it was all over! Messengers arrived to breathlessly deliver this brutal announcement: 'Your daughter is dead' (v. 35). And hope also died. R. C. H. Lenski captures it all in these crushing words: 'So Jairus had started for Jesus too late. Death outran him and won the race.'[1]

All that was left for Jairus was to go home and tend to the wretched business of burying his daughter and berating himself for not seeking Jesus sooner.

Such is the story from Jairus' point of view. But what about Jesus? Was he prepared to join Jairus in declaring the situation hopeless and walking away in resignation? Not for a moment! When others were 'throwing in the towel', Jesus was just rolling up his sleeves to go to work.

Silencing the voices of despair (vv. 35-40)

The passage calls our attention to two voices of despair.

The messengers

First, there were the messengers who brought the heart-wrenching news. We do not know whether these people were relatives or friends, but they took it upon themselves to pronounce the situation hopeless. Notice the way they put it: 'Your daughter is dead. Why trouble the Teacher any further?' (v. 35).

They assumed that Jesus couldn't do anything about death. Charles R. Erdman says their words were 'enough to quench the hope of the most ardent believer.'[2]

Where there's life, there's hope. But there was now no life. So there was no hope!

But Jesus would have none of it! Before Jairus could slide into the mire of despair, Jesus spoke boldly and decisively: 'Do not be afraid; only believe' (v. 36).

Precious words! Someone has counted 365 occurrences of 'Fear not' in the Bible. One for each day of the year!

Jairus had already shown faith by seeking out Jesus. He had disregarded what people would say about him, a ruler of the synagogue, casting himself at the feet of a man considered heretical by the religious authorities of the day.

He had come to Jesus out of deep awareness of his need and with great humility. He had shown willingness to do what Jesus said. In these ways he serves as an excellent model for all who would approach Christ. But now his faith was beginning to crumble, and he sorely needed these reassuring words from Jesus. Jesus was simply saying, 'You have believed up to this point, so don't stop now. Keep believing.'

What the gloomy messengers didn't understand, and what Jairus was about to misunderstand, was that there need be no limits placed on the power of Christ. He is just as able to raise the dead as he is to heal the sick.

The mourners

After Jesus and Jairus arrived at the house they encountered another voice of despair — that of the professional mourners who had already arrived and begun their deafening wails and shrieks. We shouldn't be surprised that they were so quickly on the scene. In those days, the dead had to be buried without delay. There was no time to lose.

The only difference between this voice and the voice of the messengers is that this was the voice of emotion while the latter was the voice of reason. When despair sets in, it always operates in both realms. It argues against all the reasons we can muster for hope, and it overwhelms our spirits.

Jesus dealt with this voice as quickly and decisively as he had with the first, meeting it head-on with these words: 'Why make this commotion and weep?' (v. 39). These words caused the voice of despair to erupt in laughter (v. 40). The mourners hooted and howled in derision. But Jesus, undaunted by the ridicule, took command of the situation by putting them all out (v. 40).

TIME OUT

◇◇◇◇◇◇◇◇◇◇◇◇◇◇◇◇◇◇◇◇◇◇◇◇◇◇

Like Jairus, we also hear voices of despair beating on our minds and slamming against our emotions. Any time we see the need for God's power, we may be sure these voices will tell us why we cannot expect to see God work.

Mention the need for revival and a chorus of voices will say the times are different, and people are too hard. Mention wanting to see loved ones saved and the voices of despair will chime in unison: 'It's no use.' Everyone who hears the voice of Christ calling him to salvation also hears the voices of despair saying, 'You are too great a sinner,' or 'You have put it off too long.'

In the midst of all these voices, Jesus says, '...only believe' (v. 36).

Listen to the voices of despair, and you will have despair. Listen to the voice of Christ and the despair will melt away and be replaced by peace, hope and joy.

Notice that Jesus didn't stop with silencing the voices of despair. That in itself was not sufficient. He had to go on to show why these voices were wrong.

Snatching the victory from death (vv. 41-43)

With the voices of despair out of the way, quietness set in. God seems to delight in doing his work with quietness and calmness and not with commotion and racket.

We are always in danger of making a great rattle and calling it God's work. We need to remember that God spoke to Elijah, not in wind, earthquake or fire, but rather in 'a gentle blowing' (1 Kings 19:12, New American Standard Version). We shall not see a true work of God until we cease our religious noise and begin relying solely on the Spirit of God (see Isa. 30:15; 32:17; Zech. 4:6).

In that atmosphere of holy calm, Jesus stepped up to the little girl, took her by the hand and said, 'Talitha, cumi' (v. 41).

Without a moment's hesitation the little girl arose and began to walk. She was completely and instantaneously restored! She wasn't even weak! Oh, the power of Christ — power to open the jaws of death and snatch away its prey!

This astounding demonstration of the power of Jesus gave notice to Satan and all his hosts that he, Jesus, would raid death of all those who believe in him.

Outside the tomb of Lazarus, on a later occasion, Jesus gave the reason for his ability to defeat death, saying, 'I am the resurrection and the life. He who believes in Me, though he may die, he shall live. And whoever lives and believes in Me shall never die' (John 11:25-26).

PAUSE TO REFLECT

Jesus has power over death because he is God. If there could be any doubt after Jesus raised others from the dead, he came out of his own grave. Paul says Jesus' resurrection proved that Christ was the Son of God (Rom. 1:4).

And with this power to conquer death, the Lord Jesus has promised to raise to everlasting life all those who trust him as Lord and Saviour (John 14:19; 1 Cor. 15:20-28).

Can you imagine the joy that flooded Jairus and his family when they saw their loved one get up and walk? What a reunion that must have been!

We don't know the details of their celebration, but we do know that all the members of God's family will be gathered to their heavenly home some glorious day.

What a day that will be! Loved ones will be reunited, tears will be wiped away, all the heavy burdens of life will melt away and despair and death will be banished for ever.

So despair and death do your utmost, but know that you will not have victory over those who know Christ!

The victory belongs to him and to his. To him belong the praise for ever and ever.

19.
A shepherd for the multitude

Mark 6:30-44

Jesus performed many 'eye-popping' miracles. He caused the deaf to hear, the blind to see and the lame to walk. He stilled storms and walked on water. He paid his taxes by having a disciple fetch a coin from a fish's mouth. He even raised three people from the dead.

It is interesting that only one of these many miracles is reported in all four Gospels — the feeding of the 5000. This miracle evidently riveted itself in the minds of the Gospel writers in a special way. Perhaps the reason is that it demonstrated the power and grace of Jesus to more eyewitnesses than any other.

Each of the four Gospels puts a slightly different slant on this miracle. Mark's particular emphasis is on Jesus as a shepherd of souls.

Jesus is the caring shepherd

Jesus had set aside a day to be with his disciples (vv. 31-32). It was intended to provide them with some much needed relaxation. But the people from the nearby towns and villages would not allow such a thing (v. 33). The one who had worked so many miracles was right there in their own area and they had to see him for themselves!

These people learned where Jesus and his disciples were going and got there ahead of them (v. 33). Mark tells us that when Jesus arrived he saw 'a great multitude' (v. 34).

But Mark tells us something else as well, namely, that Jesus was 'moved with compassion for them, because they were like sheep not having a shepherd' (v. 34).

The fact that these people were intruding into his private time did not matter. And the fact that most of them were there only to see something spectacular did not matter. Jesus began to teach and heal. He was never able to look upon the multitudes with an unfeeling, uncaring heart.

Can we identify with him at this point? Do we feel compassion for the multitudes around us? Or are we, like the priest and Levite in Jesus' parable of the Good Samaritan, content to rush right by obvious and crying needs?

Jesus is the feeding shepherd

The fact of the matter is that Jesus fed that multitude in two ways.

He first fed them spiritually. When Jesus saw the multitude, he 'began to teach them many things' (v. 34).

Jesus also fed them physically. When Jesus finished ministering, it was late. The people had not eaten, and the place was so remote that food wasn't easily attainable. The disciples suggested that Jesus send the people away so they could buy food (v. 36), but Jesus responded: 'You give them something to eat' (v. 37).

Jesus was preparing to feed these people physically, but even that physical feeding was intended to portray the spiritual feeding that he had already given them. By feeding them bread and fish he would drive home his ability to feed them with the Word of God. We must keep this in mind.

TIME OUT

People come hungering to the church. They may not realize it, but their hunger is for the Word of God. That alone can truly satisfy them.

And to her immense shame, the church often sends these hungering people away from the very food that she, the church, is charged to feed them. She sends them to entertainment, to pop-psychology, to political analyses. Meanwhile, the Lord Jesus is telling his church to feed people the Word of God!

When will the churches and their pastors ever learn that the greatest need people have is the Word of God and the gospel that that Word proclaims? The bread Jesus fed those people in the wilderness is emblematic of himself as the bread of life (John 6:35), and we can only learn about Jesus through the written Word of God.

A few minutes after discussing the situation with his disciples, Jesus used them to distribute the food that he had provided (v. 41).

We have in this a marvellous picture of what the church is to be doing. As we face the needy multitudes of our day, we must resist the temptation to create a new and novel message but simply give ourselves to faithfully distributing the message we have received from the Lord.

Jesus is the sufficient shepherd

The disciples were at a loss when Jesus told them to feed the multitude. We can imagine Philip perhaps pulling an envelope out of his pocket and furiously scratching out a calculation. It would take at least two hundred denarii worth of bread to feed these people, and with that each person would only have 'a little' (John 6:7).

The five loaves and two fishes that the disciples found (v. 38) must have seemed to them to be woefully inadequate for such a large number of people. But the Lord Jesus knew better than the disciples. He always knows better than his disciples!

After the people were seated, Jesus took the boy's lunch, gave thanks, broke it in pieces and gave it to his disciples to distribute to the people. As they distributed it, the lunch multiplied until all were fully satisfied! (v. 42).

The meal Jesus provided was more than sufficient. Twelve baskets of food were left over (v. 43) — one for each of the disciples! James Montgomery Boice wonderfully declares:

> ...the insufficient from the hands of the insignificant became sufficient and significant when placed in the hands of Jesus.[1]

The Lord has always delighted in taking small, insignificant things and making much of them.

What is the jawbone of a donkey? But the Lord enabled Samson to use it to kill a thousand of Israel's enemies.

How insignificant is a shepherd's sling! But the Lord used it to give David victory over the towering Goliath!

A shepherd for the multitude

What could be more insignificant than a Jewish peasant girl in the mighty Roman Empire? But God chose such a girl to bring Jesus into the world!

Then there is the little village of Bethlehem. How important is that? But God chose that village as the birthplace of his Son.

And outside the village are some shepherds. Nothing was more commonplace and insignificant than shepherds! But those men received a visit from the angels of heaven and heard the announcement of the Saviour's birth!

Over here now is a cross standing on a hill. The Romans were in charge in those days and it was not at all unusual to see crosses. Crucifixion was one of the ways the Romans used to control things.

Hanging on this particular cross is a Jewish rabbi who has been reared in a carpenter's shop — nothing very special about any of that!

Yet that man *was* special, and that cross was special. That man was God in human flesh, and that cross was the place where he carried out the greatest thing that has ever happened. There he received the wrath of God in the place of sinners. The Lord Jesus himself said, 'I am the good shepherd. The good shepherd gives His life for the sheep' (John 10:11).

And now the good word goes out from the pages of Scripture that all sinners who turn from their sins and embrace him as their Lord and Saviour will never have to receive that wrath themselves.

That picture of a man hanging on a cross seems to be such a minor event. The intellectual Greeks would laugh at it, and the religious Jews would scorn; but that cross was actually the expression of both the wisdom and power of God. As the apostle Paul declares: 'For the message of the cross is foolishness to those who are perishing, but to us who are being saved it is the power of God' (1 Cor. 1:18).

This is the message the church is to declare, and as she does so, she can rest assured that those who receive the message will be 'filled' (v. 42).

PAUSE TO REFLECT

The much-loved 23rd Psalm tells us that the Lord is the shepherd who makes his people to lie down in green pastures (Ps. 23:2). The pasture is the place where the sheep feed and are satisfied.

On the day described in our passage, Jesus made the multitude to sit down on 'the green grass' (v. 39), and he fed them.

He is still feeding people in the green pastures of his Word and the gospel that it proclaims. He is still our caring, feeding and sufficient shepherd.

20.
Who can this be?

◇◇

Mark 4:35-41

Our theme comes from the disciples of Jesus, who, after Jesus stilled the storm, exclaimed: 'Who can this be...!' (v. 41).

It may seem to be an odd thing to say. The man who stilled the storm was Jesus. They knew him. They had been walking with him.

But it is possible to know someone without really knowing him. Yes, the disciples knew that this was Jesus, but now they realize that there was much more to him than they could possibly comprehend.

Unbelievers urgently need to understand that there is much more to Jesus than they realize!

We believers need to understand the same. With all the knowledge we have of Jesus, we do not know enough! We have only scratched the surface. We who believe in the Lord Jesus should take as our own the words of Eliza E. Hewitt:

More about Jesus would I know,
More of His grace to others show;
More of His saving fulness see,
More of His love who died for me.

So what is the truth about Jesus that we so keenly need to understand? What does this account of Jesus stilling the storm tell us about him?

Jesus was a real man

This passage tells us that he was 'asleep on a pillow' (v. 38) when 'a great windstorm arose' (v. 37).

Why was he asleep? He was tired. And why was he tired? He was a human being, and human beings get tired!

Jesus was not God pretending to be a human being. He was not God masquerading as a man. He was both God and man at one and the same time.

Is it important that Jesus was fully man? It is supremely so! Jesus came to this earth for the express purpose of providing salvation for sinners. He could not have done this had he not been truly human. It was humanity that sinned against God. It was humanity that had to satisfy the demands of God before reconciliation between God and sinners could take place. Therefore, if Jesus had not been truly man, there would have been no salvation for anyone. We have often put it in this way: he had to be one of us in order to do something for us!

There is yet another dimension to the fact of Jesus being fully human, and it is a most blessed dimension indeed. Because Jesus was truly human, he is able to sympathize with us in weaknesses.

The author of Hebrews puts it in these words: 'For we do not have a High Priest who cannot sympathize with our weaknesses, but was in all points tempted as we are, yet without sin' (Heb. 4:15).

The humanity of Jesus not only means that he can sympathize with us; it means that he cannot help but sympathize with us. The disciples were wrong to assume that Jesus did not care about their crisis (v. 38), and we are equally wrong when we allow ourselves to think that he does not care about us and our circumstances.

TIME OUT

J. C. Ryle writes:

> The Saviour in whom we are bid to trust, is as really man as he is God. He knows the trials of a man, for He has experienced them. He knows the bodily infirmities of a man, for He has felt them. He can well understand what we mean, when we cry to Him for help in this world of need. He is just the very Saviour that men and women, with weary frames and aching heads, in a weary world, require for their comfort every morning and night.[1]

Jesus was God

We should never doubt for a moment that Jesus was fully man, but we should hold with equal force and fervour to this: he was fully God. Coming to this earth in our humanity did not diminish his deity for even a split second.

Our little and limited minds want to say that it must be one or the other. Jesus had to be God or man. But it is blessedly both. He was God and man.

The disciples had plenty of opportunities to observe the humanity of Jesus, and seeing his real humanity on such a regular and frequent basis may very well have made them think that he was only a man. But then something would happen to remind them that he was God in human flesh.

It is right here in our passage. One moment he is sleeping. That is humanity. The next moment he is standing and rebuking the wind and sea: 'Peace, be still!' (v. 39). That is not humanity! It is deity!

There are many instances of this very thing in the Gospel accounts. One moment Jesus is sitting on a well because he is weary. That is humanity! The next moment he is telling a woman everything she had ever done. That is deity! (John 4:1-29).

One moment Jesus is being arrested by Jewish authorities. That is humanity! The next moment, he identifies himself as Jesus, and those same authorities 'drew back and fell to the ground' (John 18:6). That is deity!

Now his body is being carried to the tomb. That is humanity! But on the third day that same body springs from the tomb. That is deity!

The deity of Jesus is, of course, as important as his humanity. He came to this earth to be the Mediator between God and sinners, to restore peace between them. In order to do this, he had to be able to represent both. His full humanity means he was able to represent sinners in the conflict, and his full deity means he was able to represent God in the same conflict. As both God and man, he, and he alone, is the sufficient Saviour.

There is yet another truth that emerges about Jesus from this account of him stilling the storm; namely, he is the Second Adam.

We know about the first Adam. He was the first man, and he enjoyed perfect fellowship with God and a perfect environment until that disastrous day when he chose to break the only commandment that God had given him. Everything changed after that. Nothing was the same! Adam's sin created one catastrophic result after another.

One of the results of Adam's sin was that it affected all the natural order. Before Adam sinned, he was in perfect harmony with nature. It did not resist him, and it did not threaten him in any way. But when Adam fell, nature fell with him (Gen. 3:17-19).

Some find this puzzling. Why would Adam's sin affect all of the natural order? Perhaps the answer is that God wanted to give testimony to the enormous significance of sin.

The Lord Jesus came to this earth to undo what Adam did. He came to be the Second Adam and the Last Adam (there will never be another).

Adam disobeyed God's command; Jesus perfectly obeyed. Adam refused to live in fellowship with God; Jesus lived in perfect fellowship with God. Adam refused to glorify God; Jesus never failed to glorify God in all that he said and did.

In his stilling of the storm, we must see that the Lord Jesus is functioning in his capacity as the Second Adam. Nature was rising up against the disciples and threatening them, but the Lord Jesus rose up and calmed nature. In so doing, he gloriously pictured that which he will finally complete.

A day is coming in which the Lord Jesus will finally calm all nature. The created order will be released from the horrendous grip of sin, and Jesus will usher his people into a new heaven and new earth.

That earth will be this earth restored to the beauty and glory it had before sin entered. And on that earth, God's people will raise their voices in praise to the one who came to earth while it was still in the clutches of sin. They will praise him for taking humanity without relinquishing deity so he could succeed where Adam failed.

Now we have the answer to the disciples' question: 'Who can this be?' He is Jesus: man, God and the Second Adam.

PAUSE TO REFLECT

At this point, another question arises: What have we done with Jesus? It is not enough to merely know the truth about him. We must submit to that truth, accepting Jesus as our Lord and Saviour.

21.
Labouring for what counts

◇◇◇

John 6:22-29

This passage brings us to the day after Jesus miraculously fed five thousand people in the wilderness.

Many of these people made their way to Capernaum the next day to search for Jesus. They were hoping for another meal.

TIME OUT
◇◇◇◇◇◇◇◇◇◇◇◇◇◇◇◇◇◇◇◇◇◇◇◇◇◇◇◇◇◇

Capernaum was on the north-west edge of the Sea of Galilee, about two and a half miles west of the point where the Jordan River entered. Mentioned sixteen times in the Gospels, Capernaum was chosen by Jesus as the base for his public ministry. Because it was unusually blessed by his ministry, Capernaum's rejection of him brought his own stiff and frightful sentence of judgement (Matt. 11:20-24).

Jesus, who could read people's minds as easily as we can read words, rebuked these people in no uncertain terms, telling them to get their priorities straight (vv. 26-27).

Because we can slip into mistaken priorities as easily as those people, we do well to heed the words of Jesus. There are four things in particular to notice here.

There is a certain kind of food here

We eat our physical food in order that we may sustain physical life, but Jesus speaks here of a food that 'endures to everlasting life' (v. 27). There is a kind of food, which, if eaten, will produce eternal life.

What value would you place on such food? Is it not clear that nothing in all this world can even come close to the value of this kind of food? Food that produces eternal life!

What is this food? The major part of this sixth chapter of John's Gospel is designed to answer that question. The food is none other than Jesus himself! A little later we find him saying, 'I am the living bread which came down from heaven. If anyone eats of this bread, he will live for ever...' (v. 51).

The people who followed Jesus to Capernaum had a false notion about him. They thought his purpose was to set up an earthly kingdom, and they were anxious to help him do it (v. 15). But Jesus was concerned about something of far greater value — giving people eternal life. He came to this earth to deal with the thing that deprives us of eternal life. He came to take sin out of the way so that sinners can enjoy fellowship with God for ever.

There is only one way that sin can be taken out of the way. Its penalty has to be paid. To say Jesus was here to take sin out of the way is another way of saying that he was here to pay the penalty for sin. The penalty for sin is the everlasting wrath of

God. On the cross, Jesus received the wrath of God in the place of sinners so that those sinners never have to receive that wrath themselves. That is the good news, which we call the gospel.

There is a certain way to eat this food

We know how to eat physical food, but do we know how to 'eat' Christ? (vv. 53-58).

There is only one way. We must believe in him. Jesus makes this abundantly plain. In verse 29, he says, 'This is the work of God, that you believe in Him whom He sent.'

In verse 40, he adds: 'And this is the will of Him who sent Me, that everyone who sees the Son and believes in Him may have everlasting life...'

In verse 47, he declares: 'Most assuredly, I say to you, he who believes in Me has everlasting life.'

This is the consistent and plain testimony of Scripture. The best-loved verse in all the Bible says: 'For God so loved the world that He gave His only begotten Son, that whoever believes in Him should not perish but have everlasting life' (John 3:16).

John 3:36 says, 'He who believes in the Son has everlasting life; and he who does not believe the Son shall not see life, but the wrath of God abides on him.' When Paul was asked the way of salvation by the Philippian jailer, he responded: 'Believe on the Lord Jesus Christ, and you will be saved...' (Acts 16:31).

However, we must be careful that we do not misunderstand what it means to believe. It is not simply a matter of acknowledging certain facts. It is not merely agreeing that there was once a man named Jesus who died on a Roman cross. It is not even a matter of agreeing to the assertion that Jesus arose from the dead.

It is rather a matter of committing ourselves to Christ. We can think of it in terms of marriage. We can believe in marriage intellectually, without being married. We can understand what marriage is and agree that it is a wonderful institution, but we are not married until we commit ourselves. And we are not saved by merely agreeing with the facts about Jesus, but rather by resting on those facts as the only possible way for us to stand acceptably in the presence of God. And this theme is prominent throughout the Gospel of John.

We can be certain that he is the food that produces everlasting life

Jesus told his hearers that he, Jesus, had the seal of God the Father on him (v. 27). Jesus was not speaking about these matters as someone who only had an opinion to contribute. He was speaking with special authority, as the one who had been validated and confirmed by God the Father (v. 27).

The crowd was more interested in the miracles than they were in what the miracles were intended to convey; but Jesus was not interested in people who were just interested in miracles. His miracles were signs which were designed to point to the fact that he was God in human flesh. They were not intended to call attention to themselves but to the power and glory of the one who performed them. They were designed to show that the words of Jesus about receiving eternal life can be trusted.

There is one thing in particular that keeps people from eating the food that endures to eternal life

Jesus left no room for doubt about the identity of this thing. It is labouring for the food that perishes (v. 27). In other words, it is being so occupied with temporal things that we ignore and neglect the Lord Jesus and the eternal life he gives.

What a sad and tragic thing it is to be so occupied with that which does *not* last that we miss out on what *does* last! Labouring for that which we must give up rather than for that which we can keep for ever!

Do not misunderstand Jesus. He was not telling people to give no attention at all to providing for their temporal needs. They were not just to sit down in a corner and do nothing. That was not his point at all. He was, rather, urging his hearers to not make the things of this life their chief concern and the primary object of their care. We are not to live in this world as if this world is all there is. It is not even most of all that there is!

The Lord Jesus himself put the matter in particularly powerful words: 'For what profit is it to a man if he gains the whole world, and loses his own soul? Or what will a man give in exchange for his soul?' (Matt. 16:26).

PAUSE TO REFLECT

Jesus' warning about labouring for food that perishes speaks on various levels. It speaks to us about the task of the church, which is to set Christ before people as the only way for them to have eternal life. How many church leaders have strayed from this fundamental truth! How many have turned church services and classes into a forum for discussing the problems of this life, which, no matter how great they are, will soon pass away. Pastors and teachers who focus entirely on temporal concerns are calling for their hearers to labour for that which is perishing.

Jesus' warning about labouring for temporal things also speaks powerfully to those who hear the gospel message. Labour to understand it! Labour to appreciate it! Labour with the realization that your very life is at stake — your eternal life!

Young people may very well need this word more than anyone else. Eternal life through Christ is set before them, but they want to act as if they are above it all. Not wanting their friends to think that they are not 'cool', they do not listen at all, or listen only in the most casual sort of way. All the while, they are gambling with their souls!

More tragic yet are those who claim to have received Christ but show no interest in him! They claim to have eaten the food that endures to eternal life, but they would not want to give the impression that they have been deeply affected by this or that they are much interested in it! Are such people not horribly deceived?

May God have mercy on all who are setting aside the message of eternal life so they can run after the perishing things of this world! May God show them in a powerful way the supreme value of eternal life! May God help all of us to join Simon Peter, who, while multitudes were walking away from Jesus, wonderfully declared: 'Lord, to whom shall we go? You have the words of eternal life' (v. 68).

22.
A supernatural disclosure

Matthew 16:13-20

To disclose something means to unveil or to uncover it so that it is plain and clear. It means something that was closed to us is closed no longer. It is now open and accessible.

There is a disclosure in these verses. It is a disclosure about Jesus, given by God himself through Simon Peter. It came when Peter said to Jesus, 'You are the Christ, the Son of the living God' (v. 16).

To appreciate and understand this disclosure we must examine its background, its meaning, its source, and its far-reaching implications or significance.

The background of this disclosure (vv. 13-15)

Jesus and his disciples were at Caesarea Philippi, a town in the north-east portion of Palestine. The name of this town tells us something of its significance. 'Caesarea' linked it with the Roman emperor, and it was the site of a temple dedicated to worshipping him. It was also a centre for the worship of other gods (the Syrian Baal, the Greek god 'Pan').

Caesarea Philippi was the site that Jesus selected to put a crucial question to his disciples: 'Who do men say that I, the Son of Man, am?' (v. 13).

There was no shortage of opinions about Jesus. Some thought he was the reincarnation of John the Baptist. Some, thinking of the last words of the Old Testament (Mal. 4:5-6), suggested that he was Elijah. Others observed in him the character of Jeremiah, the weeping prophet, and assumed that he was Jeremiah returned to life. Still others suggested that he was the reincarnation of one of the other great prophets in Israel's history.

After hearing these responses, the Lord Jesus proceeded to sharpen the question. He wasn't about to let the disciples take refuge in the popular thinking of the day. So he asked: 'But who do you say that I am?' (v. 15).

Simon Peter was equal to the occasion. Without hesitation, he firmly asserted: 'You are the Christ, the Son of the living God' (v. 16).

The meaning of this disclosure (v. 16)

This was no small thing that Simon asserted. The word 'Christ' means 'anointed one'. It was not Jesus' middle (or last) name! It is rather a reference to his office or function. He was anointed of God to perform the threefold function of prophet, priest and king. As prophet, he represents God to men by declaring the truth of God. As priest, he represents men to God, that is, providing access to God through his atoning death. As king, he rules and reigns over the citizens of his kingdom, which is a spiritual kingdom.

In asserting that Jesus was 'the Son of the living God,' Peter was affirming that Jesus was no mere man, but rather was God in human flesh. Unlike the pagan deities celebrated at Caesarea Philippi, Jesus had the eternal life of God in himself (and, recalling John 6:68-69, we can say Jesus was able to grant eternal life to others).

The source of this disclosure (v. 17)

This was a tremendous affirmation from the lips of Simon Peter, but the Lord Jesus did not want his disciple to feel inflated with his own wisdom and insight. He, therefore, immediately let him and the other disciples know that this insight was heaven-born. It was God who had enabled Simon to see the truth about Jesus. Salvation is ever the result of the grace of God opening blind eyes to see the truth.

This enabling work of God made Simon a 'blessed' or 'happy' man. We have all sorts of ways to measure happiness today. Here is how Jesus measured it — the truly happy person is the one who has been enabled to see Jesus as the Christ, the Son of the living God.

The significance of this disclosure (vv. 18-20)

After pointing out the source of Simon's knowledge, the Lord Jesus proceeded to declare the far-reaching significance of his statement. The truth Simon had just uttered was the foundation stone of the church that Jesus was going to build.

Jesus responded to Peter's glowing confession of faith by using a play on words: essentially he said, 'You are "Petros" (a little rock), but I am going to build my church on "petra" (a big rock)'.

In other words, Peter, the little rock, had given expression to something that was truly big, something so gigantic, massive and firm that the church could be built upon it, namely, the truth about the Lord Jesus.

In addition to this, the Lord gave to Simon Peter (and the other disciples) the 'keys of the kingdom'. Taking the truth about Jesus, they would have the authority to bind and loose. If someone refused the truth about Christ, they had the authority to say this person was still bound in his sins. If one accepted the truth about Christ, these men had the right to say he had been loosed from his sins.

PAUSE TO REFLECT

People are as much 'up in the air' about Jesus as they were when Jesus asked his disciples: 'Who do men say that I, the Son of Man, am?' (v. 13).

The truth about Jesus has not changed since that ancient day. He is the same Christ that Simon Peter proclaimed him to be. We must make sure we are not mistaken about Jesus because eternal salvation rests entirely on him.

Simon certainly spoke the truth about Jesus when he called him the Christ and the Son of the living God (v. 16), but it was Simon's truth only in a secondary fashion. Simon Peter had not come to it because he had a superior mind and because he exerted that mind in a superior fashion. He rather came to the truth only because God gave it to him.

That which was true of Simon Peter on this occasion is still true today. We do not naturally know the truth about God and his way of salvation (1 Cor. 2:14). By nature our minds are darkened (2 Cor. 4:4).

How, then, does anyone ever come to the truth? Only through the grace of God! (Eph. 2:8-9). God graciously enables us to understand the truth about him (he is the holy God before whom we must give account) and about ourselves (we are responsible to honour him by living in obedience to his commands and we have failed to do this). God also graciously enables us to understand that he has provided in Jesus the way for our sins to be forgiven so we can stand acceptably in his presence.

Everyone who gets to heaven will know how he got there. No one will take credit for himself. Each one will give testimony to the grace of God that both gave the truth and the mind to understand the truth.

23.
Contradictory proclamations

Matthew 16:21-23

The Lord God himself first announced the cross of Christ to Adam and Eve after they fell into sin. He announced that the seed of the woman, the Lord Jesus (Gal. 4:4), would crush the serpent's head (Gen. 3:15). From the time of that announcement, the serpent (Satan) knew about the cross. We cannot go into detail about how much he knew and how much he did not know. We do not have the line to fathom that depth. There were times in which Satan, as we are about to discover, seemed to pull out all the stops to prevent Jesus from going to the cross. But, strangely enough, there were also times in which he used the wicked plots of wicked men to drive Jesus to the cross. There is a tension in his position that can only be explained in eternity.

TIME OUT

◇◇◇◇◇◇◇◇◇◇◇◇◇◇◇◇◇◇◇◇◇◇◇◇◇◇◇◇◇◇

The Old Testament is the account of God moving toward the fulfilment of his promise to send his Son. It is simultaneously the account of Satan feverishly working to thwart the promise. It is the account of the dragon seeking to devour the child (Rev. 12:1-6).

It often looked as if Satan would succeed. God determined that Israel would be the nation through which his Son would come. So Satan focused on destroying that nation. Her years of bondage in Egypt and, centuries later, her seventy years of captivity in Babylon are two such attempts.

God also determined that his Son would be a descendant of King David. So Satan also sought to destroy that line. It appeared from time to time that he would succeed there too. Queen Athaliah's attempt to destroy the Davidic line (2 Kings 11; 2 Chron. 22 & 23) and the Babylonian Captivity constituted major threats, but the line of David survived both, and the Lord Jesus arrived on the stage of human history in 'the fulness of the time' (Gal. 4:4). Jesus came, and he wasn't even late!

At Caesarea Philippi, Satan's mind was very much on diverting Jesus from the cross.

The proclamation of Jesus (v. 21)

The content of his proclamation

Here we have Jesus proclaiming his death. His words give evidence of very complete and thorough knowledge. His death would be in Jerusalem, and it would be at the hands of the religious leaders. It would also feature many sufferings.

His words also give evidence of his sense of appointment. He 'must go' to Jerusalem. Some mistakenly think that Jesus came to this earth with the intention of offering himself to his people as their earthly king. Supposedly surprised by their rejection of him, Jesus had to 'fall back' to the cross. In this scheme, the cross was 'Plan B'.

This is all wrong. The Bible tells us that Jesus was 'the Lamb slain from the foundation of the world' (Rev. 13:8).

The cross was in the mind and heart of God before the world began, and Jesus came to this earth with his eye fixed on that cross and for the express purpose of going there. His Father had made an appointment with him and that cross, and Jesus would not allow anything to keep him from that appointment.

The place of his proclamation

It is interesting that Jesus spoke about his impending death while he was at Caesarea Philippi. As we have already mentioned, its very name tells us that it was a centre for worship of the Roman Caesar. It was also a centre of worship for the Syrian Baal and the Greek god 'Pan'.

This, then, was the place of religious pluralism. It was the perfect place for Jesus to say something along these lines: 'You see, there are many religions, and each has its own special and distinct contribution to make, and each is valid. We must be glad for this pluralism and let it enrich our lives.'

It is quite significant that Jesus deliberately chose the place of religious diversity to proclaim a narrow message. He claimed to be the Messiah (vv. 16-17) who had come to die on the cross (v. 21). He further claimed that he was the one whom others should follow (v. 24), and their refusal to do so would result in them losing their souls (v. 26).

The proclamation of Satan (v. 22)

No sooner had Jesus delivered the message about his forthcoming death on the cross than Satan stepped up to object. He did so by using Simon Peter to say, 'Far be it from You, Lord; this shall not happen to You!' (v. 22).

This is a sad thing. Simon Peter is scant moments away from having brilliantly confessed the truth about Jesus: 'You are the Christ, the Son of the living God' (v. 16).

Let us learn from this how very weak and feeble the saints of God are, and how very quickly they can stumble and tumble!

What a remarkable sight we have here! Jesus speaks about the cross, and Simon takes him by the arm, steers him aside — as a parent might a child! — and tells him, Jesus, that he is mistaken! If he would listen to himself for a split second, he would realize his folly: 'Far be it from You, Lord...' In one breath, he both calls Jesus 'Lord' and tells him he is wrong! It always sounds strange when a servant says, 'No, Lord.'

Part of Jesus' messiahship was the role of prophet, that is, one who declares the truth of God. Simon Peter has just declared him to be the Messiah, but when he, Jesus, functions as the Messiah, Simon objects. He talks and acts as if he knows more than the Christ! The scene drips with irony.

What was Satan's purpose in using Simon? It was, as we have already noted, to divert Jesus from the cross. Satan clearly regarded a crucified Christ as the ultimate disaster for his kingdom. Now if Satan regards the crucified Christ in such a way, should we not regard that same Christ in exactly the opposite way. If the crucified Christ was Satan's nightmare, should he not be our glory? How many of us are actually glorying in this Christ?

The response of Jesus (v. 23)

How does Jesus respond to Simon's rebuke? Does he congratulate him on his insight and thank him for his contribution? Not at all! He rebukes him in no uncertain terms: 'Get behind Me, Satan! You are an offence to Me, for you are not mindful of the things of God, but the things of men.'

So Jesus both identified the cross as 'the things of God' and all those who oppose it as 'Satan'.

And he reminded Simon Peter that the proper place for the disciple is always behind his master. The disciple is to follow, not lead! Satan had got behind Simon and pushed him out in front of Jesus to lead, and Jesus is now pushing Simon back to his rightful place.

By the way, there is tremendous comfort in the Lord Jesus exposing Satan by rebuking Simon. This shows us that the preaching of the cross will not perish from the earth. No matter how Satan attacks, he will never be able to destroy the saving message of the cross.

PAUSE TO REFLECT

Centuries have come and gone since that ancient day in Caesarea Philippi, but little has changed. The Lord Jesus is still sending his message out into this world. It is still the message of his cross. He declares that no one can stand acceptably in the presence of the holy God unless his sins are forgiven, and the only way for sins to be forgiven is through that cross. The Lord Jesus tells us that he died there in the place of sinners. He took their penalty, the penalty of separation from God, so that those sinners who will come to him in repentance and faith will not have to endure that penalty themselves.

Satan is also sending out his message. It is the message that scorns and ridicules that cross. Every time a minister stands in a pulpit to minimize the cross or to in any way deny it, Satan's leering face can be seen behind him.

The two messages still go out, and the choice still remains. Will we listen to the message of the cross, or the message that despises it? And let those who dare stand in pulpits answer this question: Will we preach the crucified Christ, or will we preach as if we know more than the one we call 'Lord'?

24.

The transfiguration of Jesus

◇◇◇

Matthew 17:1-9

Our word 'transfiguration' comes from the Greek word 'metamorphoomai', from which we get the word 'metamorphosis'.

When something 'metamorphoses' it undergoes a striking change in appearance or character.

The transfiguration and the person of Christ

TIME OUT
◇◇◇◇◇◇◇◇◇◇◇◇◇◇◇◇◇◇◇◇◇◇◇◇◇◇◇

Scripture tells us the Lord Jesus Christ was transfigured before three of his disciples. R. C. Sproul gets at the essence of what happened with these words: 'The prefix trans- means literally "across". In the transfiguration a limit or barrier is crossed. We

TIME OUT

◇◇◇◇◇◇◇◇◇◇◇◇◇◇◇◇◇◇◇◇◇◇◇◇◇◇◇◇◇◇

might call it a crossing of the line between the natural and the supernatural, between the human and the divine. It crosses a boundary of dimensions into the realm of God.'[1]

In the presence of Peter, James and John, the Lord Jesus crossed that barrier between the human and the divine. He was substantially changed. While he was still very much a part of earth, he took on a heavenly appearance.

Charles Erdman sums it up in this way: 'It is as if the monarch had been walking in disguise; only occasionally beneath his humble garment has been revealed a glimpse of the purple and the gold. Here, for an hour, the disguise is withdrawn and the King appears in his real majesty and in the regal splendor of his divine glory.'[2]

When the second person of the Trinity took our humanity, he did not cease to be God. That deity was still there, but it was veiled. In the transfiguration, the veil was, as it were, drawn back so that the deity that was always there could be seen clearly.

It was an amazing sight. Matthew says Jesus' face 'shone like the sun, and His clothes became as white as the light' (Matt. 17:2).

Mark says, 'His clothes became shining, exceedingly white, like snow, such as no launderer on earth can whiten them' (Mark 9:3).

Luke adds this word: '...the appearance of His face was altered, and His robe became white and glistening' (Luke 9:29).

R. C. Sproul sums it up in this terse comment: 'The glory of Christ perhaps never became more evident than at His transfiguration.'[3]

The sight of the transfigured Christ was astounding enough in and of itself, but the Scriptures include another astounding thing, namely, Moses and Elijah also appeared as glorified beings and talked with him.

Why Moses and Elijah? Kent Hughes answers:

Both these men had previously conversed with God on mountaintops — Moses on Mt. Sinai (Exodus 31:18) and Elijah on Mt. Horeb (1 Kings 19:9ff.). These both had been shown God's glory. Both also had famous departures from this earth. Moses died on Mt. Nebo, and God had buried him in a grave known only to himself. Elijah was taken up in a chariot of fire. Moses was the great lawgiver, and Elijah was the great prophet. Moses was the founder of Israel's religious economy, and Elijah was the restorer of it. Together they were an ultimate summary of the Old Testament economy.[4]

Christ transfigured and appearing with the glorified Moses and Elijah! What was it all about? Scripture doesn't leave us to our own speculations.

The transfiguration and the work of Christ

It should not escape our attention that each of the three Gospel accounts contains a distinct reference to the timing of the transfiguration. Matthew and Mark are very precise: it was six days after Jesus predicted — and Peter contradicted — his death (Matt. 17:1; Mark 9:2). Luke, on the other hand, is content to approximate the time, 'about eight days' (Luke 9:28).

The fact that each of the Gospel writers relates the transfiguration to what had taken place at Caesarea Philippi indicates that we are to interpret it in the light of what transpired there.

The fact that the discussion at Caesarea Philippi centred on Jesus' death on the cross means the transfiguration must be related to that cross. Luke makes this connection clear by saying that the transfigured Christ discussed with Moses and Elijah 'His decease which He was about to accomplish at Jerusalem' (Luke 9:31).

It is striking that Jesus' death is spoken of as something that he was going to 'accomplish' rather than suffer. Jesus wasn't just a passive victim when he died there on Calvary's cross. He was actively pursuing the plan that he and the Father had agreed upon. He knew in advance that this was going to happen. He went up that mountain with the awareness that he was going to be transfigured and that he would meet Moses and Elijah. By going there, he was affirming the cross upon which he and the Father had agreed in eternity past.

The whole episode came to a conclusion with the Father again speaking from heaven, 'This is My beloved Son. Hear Him!' (Luke 9:35). By his presence there on the mount, the Son was affirming the cross, and by speaking from heaven, the Father was affirming his Son. Father and Son were still together on the matter of the cross.

But the words of the Father must also be related to Caesarea Philippi. There the Lord Jesus clearly predicted for his disciples in a very explicit manner that his messiahship meant execution at the hands of the religious leaders. And there Peter, after confessing in a sterling manner the deity of the Lord Jesus, took it upon himself to contradict his Lord.

We can imagine Simon Peter stewing and fretting during those days after Caesarea Philippi. Had he been right to proclaim Jesus as the Son of God? How could the Son of God die at the hands of wicked men? How could such a Messiah possibly fulfil the Old Testament prophecies?

Six days after his befuddlement set in, Peter had his answer. The fact that Jesus took on a heavenly appearance proved indisputably that he was the Son of God from heaven. And his appearing there with Moses and Elijah to talk specifically about his death indicated that a dying Messiah was exactly what the law and the prophets had envisioned.

At Caesarea Philippi Simon Peter gives evidence of eroded faith. He had by this time been associated with Jesus for so long and on such an intimate basis that he no longer felt the sense of awe and wonder he once did. Prolonged association with Christ had eroded the awe he had felt when the Lord called him to be a disciple (Luke 5:8). There was, therefore, a readiness on his part to lecture Jesus and to dispute with him.

There was to be yet another faltering step for Peter. While he was basking in the glow of transfigured glory, he blurted out, 'Master, it is good for us to be here; and let us make three tabernacles: one for You, one for Moses, and one for Elijah' (Luke 9:33).

That was definitely a faltering step. It not only placed the Lord Jesus on the same level as Moses and Elijah, but it also sought to perpetuate the experience. And that, of course, meant stopping short of the cross.

Such was Peter's ill-considered response to the transfiguration, although it is safe to say that the transfiguration forcefully brought the awe of Christ back to Simon Peter. There he and the others were made to realize afresh that Jesus was not just a mere man who could be mistaken and needed to be corrected, but was God in flesh. And, therefore, what he had to say about his approaching death must be accepted.

Glyn Owen says the transfiguration changed Peter's mind about the cross: 'He learned that God knows better. He learned that Moses and Elijah know better. He learned that heaven knows better than earth.'[5]

Then Owen adds this word of application: 'Blessed is the man who can change his mind like that, in accordance with heavenly understanding.'[6]

PAUSE TO REFLECT

The transfiguration of Jesus must certainly be classified as one of the most powerful and moving experiences that Peter, James and John had during their years of association with Jesus. While we should rejoice that these men were given this experience, we must not think that we need a similar experience to be sure about our faith. The same apostle Peter who saw Jesus transfigured tells us that we can be certain about Jesus because of the sure testimony of Scripture (2 Peter 1:19-21).

25.
A boy suffering from seizures

◇◇◇

Mark 9:14-29

Now we accompany Jesus as he comes down from the Mount of Transfiguration, and we find him dealing with a young lad who was demon-possessed.

We might say that Jesus had a whole series of appointments as he was moving toward his main appointment with the cross. One of those appointments was with this poor boy.

This story is not here merely to entertain us but to remind us that Jesus was the God-man and to call us to faith in him. We can say that it is here to cause us to stand in awe of the Lord Jesus. We have noticed that prolonged contact with Jesus can cause our sense of awe to erode. That is what happened with Simon Peter, causing him to be quick to reprimand Jesus (Matt. 16:22-23). The same can happen to us!

Let us pray, then, that the Lord will use our consideration of Jesus' dealings with this demon-possessed boy to restore awe to our needy hearts.

We can divide this account into two major considerations. First, we see the sad situation; and then, the sufficient Saviour.

The sad situation (vv. 14-18)

The sadness of the situation consists of three elements.

The demon-possessed boy (vv. 17-18, 20-22)

Few biblical stories are more heart-wrenching. The demon that possessed this boy had not only rendered him mute, but often caused him to have convulsions in which he wallowed on the ground, foaming at the mouth, gnashing his teeth and becoming rigid (v. 18). At times the demon had caused the boy to fall into the fire or into water (v. 22).

The powerless disciples (v. 18)

The father, at the end of his tether, had brought his son, we assume, to Jesus. But when he arrived, Jesus was on the Mount of Transfiguration with Peter, James and John. The father, then, did the next best thing, which was to present his situation to the disciples who were present. These men, who had cast out demons on previous occasions (6:7,13), were unable to cast out this demon.

TIME OUT

◇◇◇◇◇◇◇◇◇◇◇◇◇◇◇◇◇◇◇◇◇◇◇◇◇

J. C. Ryle offers these words of wisdom:

> Let us learn a lesson of humility from the failure of the disciples. Let us strive to realize every day our need of the grace and presence of Christ. With Him we may do all

TIME OUT

things. Without Him we can do nothing at all. With Him we may overcome the greatest temptations. Without Him the least may overcome us. Let our cry be every morning, 'leave us not to ourselves — we know not what a day may bring forth — if thy presence go not with us we cannot go up.'[1]

The disdainful critics (vv. 14-18)

The failure of the disciples caused the religious leaders who happened to be present to enter into 'disputing' with the disciples (v. 14). In this context the word 'disputing' should probably be taken to mean that the scribes were having a very good time at the expense of the disciples as they mocked and ridiculed them.

The three elements of this sad situation are very much present today. Like the disciples of old, we find ourselves up against the tyranny of Satan in its many forms — tyranny so powerful that it is wrecking bodies, minds, homes, churches and every part of our society. And like the disciples, the church today seems utterly powerless to stem the tide of wickedness and to overcome the power of Satan.

In addition to all this, we are surrounded by those who look with disdain upon Christianity, mock our message and ridicule our efforts.

We should be thankful that we do not have to leave it at that.

The sufficient Saviour (vv. 19-27)

The situation seemed to be hopeless, but Jesus cast the demon out of the boy and brought the father to faith in himself.

This part of Mark's account can be divided into three sections. Firstly, Jesus addresses the assembly. Secondly, he addresses the father. Finally, he addresses the demon.

Jesus addresses the assembly (v. 19)

Jesus, Peter, James and John returned from the mount to the scene of frustration and turmoil we have noted. The hearts of the nine disciples must have leaped with joy as they saw Jesus walking toward them. Jesus immediately took the situation in hand. After asking the scribes why they were disputing with his disciples (v. 16) and after the father explained his situation (v. 18), Jesus offered this word of rebuke: 'O faithless generation, how long shall I be with you? How long shall I bear with you?' (v. 19). To whom was this rebuke addressed? William Hendriksen answers by saying of Jesus:

> He was evidently deeply dissatisfied with his contemporaries: with the father, who lacked sufficient faith in Christ's healing power (9:22-24); with the scribes, who, instead of showing any pity, were in all probability gloating over the disciples' impotence (9:14); with the crowd in general, which is pictured in the Gospels as being generally far more concerned about itself than about others (John 6:26); and, last but not least, with the nine disciples, because of their failure to exercise their faith by putting their whole heart into persevering prayer (9:29).[2]

Jesus addresses the father (vv. 20-24)

While the young man was wallowing on the ground and foaming at the mouth, the father in his anguish said to Jesus, 'But if You can do anything, have compassion on us and help us' (vv. 20-22).

What a daring assertion! This man thought failure to cast out the demon would be due to Jesus' lack of ability. Jesus made it clear that failure would not be due to this but rather to the father's lack of faith (v. 23).

It was not that Jesus needed this man's faith to cast out this demon — as if his power can somehow be increased by faith or diminished by lack of it — but rather that Jesus had determined that, as a general rule, faith would be the channel through which his power flowed.

Jesus' words immediately caused the man to see how wrong he had been to attribute some deficiency to Jesus. His cry, 'Lord, I believe; help my unbelief!' (v. 24), was at one and the same time a confession of faith in Christ and a confession that his faith, while real, was weak and needed to be strengthened.

Jesus addresses the demon (vv. 25-27)

Having heard this confession, the Lord turned his attention to the demon that was possessing the young man and said, 'I command you, come out of him and enter him no more!' (v. 25).

This was no mere man who issued this command. It was none other than the Lord of glory clothed in human flesh, the one who has supreme authority.

The demon had no choice but to give up his possession of the young man.

PAUSE TO REFLECT

What does all this have to do with us? Why have we even taken the time to consider this ancient episode? The answer should be obvious. The same powerful Christ who delivered this man works on behalf of feeble and helpless people today!

Every child of God is a testimony to this. We were once completely incapacitated by sin. But the sufficient Saviour came in to heal us of our sin and make us whole.

That same Saviour is still saving sinners today. Therefore, if you are not a believer in Christ, run to Jesus and receive the salvation that he alone provides.

26.
A gracious invitation

John 7:37-44

Jesus spoke these words on the final day of the Feast of Tabernacles in Jerusalem, which was the last and most elaborate of the seven feasts which the Jews observed each year. Its purpose was to re-enact their fathers' wilderness wanderings. To do this, the people erected and stayed in temporary booths. They also engaged in a dramatic water-pouring ceremony each day. This commemorated God's miraculous provision of water in the wilderness (Exod. 17:6; Num. 20:11).

On each of the seven feast days water was drawn in a golden pitcher from the pool of Siloam and carried in a grand procession to the temple. There it was poured out on the altar. On the seventh day, 'that great day of the feast', there were seven processions around the altar.

Throughout these ceremonies the excitement of the people would build until it was at fever-pitch on the last day. Then it would all be over. The people would dismantle their booths and depart for their homes, a picture of their fathers entering 'a land of springs and waters', that is, a land of permanent dwellings. We should not be surprised if the jubilation of the feast soon gave way to a keen sense of dissatisfaction. These people may very well have come away from the feast realizing that the ceremonies had not really satisfied their deepest yearnings. Participating in water-pouring ceremonies alone could not satisfy the thirst within for God and for forgiveness of sins.

It was probably after the final ceremony, when the first pangs of dissatisfaction may have set in, that the people were startled with Jesus' cry: 'If anyone thirsts, let him come to Me and drink.'

A grievous condition

Jesus captured the attention of the multitude with the word 'thirst', which carried a great deal of significance for the Jews. Much of their history was bound up in the need for water. Abraham, Isaac and Jacob found it necessary to constantly move their flocks in search of water. Later, King Hezekiah had to perform a staggering feat of engineering in order to provide water when Jerusalem was under siege (2 Chron. 32:3-4).

The word 'thirst' also carried great spiritual significance. The psalmist David had used it to depict his desire for God: 'My soul thirsts for God, for the living God...' (Ps. 42:2).

Again, David wrote: 'My soul thirsts for You; my flesh longs for You in a dry and thirsty land' (Ps. 63:1).

In each case David was expressing a continual, intense longing for God. The people of Jesus' day were aware of David's words. When Jesus said, 'If anyone thirsts', they knew what he meant. He could just as well have said, 'If any man has a deep longing for God, let him come to Me.'

This word continues to have great relevance. I dare say it is the most appropriate word to describe what multitudes are experiencing at this moment. I'm not saying that they are conscious of a hunger for God, but I am convinced that they are conscious of a deep dissatisfaction, an insatiable desire for something.

If you were to suggest that they need God, they would dismiss it as utter nonsense. Instead they try everything else, thinking that something will surely satisfy. Pleasure is tried and fails. Possessions fail. It's the same with prestige and power. All fail.

Others appear to realize that it is God they need. The question for them is how to find him. They try various religions, philosophies and cults, but their thirst remains because God is not automatically identified with any one particular religion or philosophy.

TIME OUT

Augustine was one who tried almost all these things. He lived a life of promiscuity, and all the while he had this 'thirst'. He also tried religion and philosophy, but the 'thirst' remained. Finally, he came to faith in Jesus Christ and the 'thirst' was quenched. Later, Augustine said to the Lord: 'Thou madest us for Thyself, and our heart is restless, until it repose in Thee.'[1]

So the word 'thirst' captures the plight of man, and it is a grievous condition indeed. But the word 'thirst' only arrested the attention of the multitude.

A gracious provision

Jesus himself was that for which the people were thirsting. So his appeal was for them to come to him and drink. Several things about his appeal are noteworthy.

It was an extensive appeal

Jesus addressed it to 'anyone'. Who doesn't know the pain of not being invited to a special event? It hurts to be slighted. The wonderful thing about God is that he doesn't slight anybody. All are invited to come and receive satisfaction for what they so desperately desire.

God is so earnest in extending his invitation to all that it is repeated time after time (Isa. 1:18; 55:1-3; Matt. 11:28-30; 22:1-14). In fact, in the last chapter of the Bible we find the words: 'And let him who thirsts come. Whoever desires, let him take the water of life freely' (Rev. 22:17).

It appears as if God refused to close the Bible without issuing one more appeal to all to come.

It was an exclusive appeal

Notice that Jesus says, 'let him come to Me.' Jesus doesn't call men to be religious or moral, but rather to come to him. Perhaps there is nothing about Christianity that so antagonizes modern man as this dogmatism. We like to think that all religions have equal value. Countless times it has been said, 'All religions are shooting for the same place and all will make it by and by.'

Where do people get such a notion? Certainly not from Jesus. He is the one who said, 'I am the way, the truth, and the life. No one comes to the Father except through Me' (John 14:6).

It was an instructive appeal

Jesus said, 'Come to Me and drink.' Coming and drinking simply mean believing in Christ. On an earlier occasion, Jesus said, '... he who believes in Me shall never thirst' (John 6:35).

Believing on Christ means consciously and deliberately resting on Christ as the sole hope for salvation. Just as drinking is the means of appropriating water for our bodies, believing is the means of appropriating Christ for our souls.

It was an attractive appeal

Jesus said, 'out of his heart will flow rivers of living water.' When a person believes in Jesus Christ, he both finds his own thirst quenched and he becomes a means of quenching the thirst of others. How attractive is that?

At this point John adds a word of explanation. He says Jesus' words were a prophecy of the coming of the Holy Spirit, who came in fulness upon believers on the Day of Pentecost after Christ had returned to the Father. On that occasion, believers became flaming witnesses for Christ. They became channels of blessing, carrying the living water of Christ to others who were thirsting.

This is the reason we find the Old Testament prophesying the coming of the Holy Spirit in terms of the issuing forth of streams of blessing:

'For I will pour water on him who is thirsty,
And floods on the dry ground;
I will pour My Spirit on your descendants,
And My blessing on your offspring;
They will spring up among the grass
Like willows by the watercourses'

(Isa. 44:3-4).

It was a divisive appeal (vv. 40-44)

It is impossible to be neutral in the face of such startling words. The words of Christ caused great ferment and division among his hearers. Some were captivated by Christ and spoke a good word for him (vv. 40-42) but that was all.

Others were prejudiced against Christ. They knew the Messiah would come out of Bethlehem, but they mistakenly assumed Jesus was from Galilee (vv. 41-42). They were the prototypes of all those who reject Christ without investigating his claims or giving him a fair hearing.

Still others were enraged against Christ to the point of wanting to kill him (v. 44).

These were their responses. Christ's appeal demands response from us also. It's not a question of whether we will respond, but which response will be ours. I hope you won't choose any of the responses of Jesus' hearers on that day. Let your response be that of true faith.

PAUSE TO REFLECT

All my life long I had panted for a
   drink from some full spring,
That I hoped would quench the burning
   of the thirst that I felt within.

Feeding on the husks around me until
   my strength was almost gone.
Longed my soul for something better,
   only still to hunger on.

Hallelujah, I have found Him,
   who my soul so long has craved.
Jesus satisfied all my longings,
   through His blood I now am saved.

27.
Truth from a trap

◇◇◇◇◇◇◇◇◇◇◇◇◇◇◇◇◇◇◇◇◇◇◇◇◇◇◇◇◇◇◇◇◇◇◇◇◇◇◇

John 8:2-12

These verses deal with the morning after the conclusion of the Feast of Tabernacles. Having spent the night on the Mount of Olives, Jesus returned early in the morning to the temple in Jerusalem where he began teaching.

Suddenly the scribes and Pharisees burst in with a woman whom they claimed had been caught in the act of adultery.

They were posing as great champions of the law of Moses, but the truth of the matter is that they had very little interest in justice. Their primary concern was to set a trap for Jesus.

More specifically, they were trying to put Jesus into a dilemma from which he could not escape without discrediting himself. Such was their intense dislike for him! Gordon Keddie is correct in saying: 'Jesus is the one who is really on trial.'[1]

The trap

Their plan was very clever indeed. It was constructed in such a way that Jesus would have to endorse or embrace one truth he had been emphasizing and repudiate another.

On one hand, he had shown great respect for the law of Moses and had said that he had not come to destroy but rather to fulfil it. On the other hand, he had shown an eagerness to forgive those who failed to keep the law.

The piercing question posed by this episode is this: how could Jesus both honour the law and let a law-breaker go free?

These religious leaders, always eager to pose as zealous guardians of the law, often disregarded the very law they professed to revere. This was the case here. The law required the following for a case such as this:

1. that there be multiple witnesses;
2. that these witnesses bring both the man and the woman before the Sanhedrin Court;
3. that the witnesses be the first to stone the man and woman if they were found guilty by the court.

It is obvious that very little of what the law required was actually being observed here. No witnesses are identified. The religious leaders simply say that the woman was 'caught in adultery' (v. 4).

The guilty man is not mentioned anywhere. And the woman is presented, not to the court, but to Jesus.

This passage highlights the selective obedience of the religious leaders. They professed to be champions of the law, but they kept only those parts that suited them. In this case they had broken the very law they were claiming to keep. These are the same men who had earlier violated the law by seeking to kill Jesus (7:19).

The religious leaders must have felt very proud of themselves. They thought Jesus could only do one of two things — call for the woman to be stoned, showing he really had no compassion for sinners; or call for the woman to be freed, showing he had no regard for the law.

As they waited with eager anticipation for Jesus to choose, he merely leaned over and wrote something on the ground (v. 6). There has been much speculation about what he wrote. It has often been suggested that Jesus wrote the names and the sins of the woman's accusers! That would certainly have put the cat among the pigeons! But while this idea makes sense and carries a lot of appeal, we simply cannot say what Jesus wrote. If the Holy Spirit had wanted us to know, he would have included it in this passage.

When the religious leaders pressed for an answer to their question, Jesus said, 'He who is without sin among you, let him throw a stone at her first' (v. 7). He then wrote again on the ground (v. 8).

When he looked up the woman alone remained. All her accusers had left (v. 9). What wonderful words Jesus spoke to her: 'Neither do I condemn you; go and sin no more' (v. 11).

S. G. DeGraaf writes:

> The grace of God burst into the woman's life. She was an outcast; she had deserved to die. However, the Lord Jesus revealed to her that we are all under the guilt of our sins, but through God there is forgiveness.[2]

What did Jesus do here? On one hand, he honoured the law by insisting that every aspect of it be kept and not just one part. By not calling for this woman to be stoned, the Lord Jesus was essentially saying, 'The law must be fully, not partially, kept.'

Gordon J. Keddie writes: 'Jesus was not here abrogating any law of God respecting sexual sin. He was in fact upholding that law. He was insisting upon rules of evidence and equal justice.'[3]

On the other hand, he showed compassion for the woman by setting her free. But in letting her go, he did not condone her sin (v. 11).

The truth

Jesus' dealings with the religious leaders and the adulterous woman have far more to do with us than we might think. They picture for us the truth of the gospel.

The law of God justly accuses each and every one of us of having broken it and of being worthy of eternal death.

The great question is this: How can God at one and the same time satisfy his law and let guilty sinners go free?

Jesus' death on the cross is God's answer to that dilemma. Through that death, God both satisfies his law and forgives sinners. God's law says the sinner must suffer eternal death for his sins. Jesus suffered on the cross an eternity's worth of wrath. The law is satisfied, then, because the penalty it demands was paid.

But the cross also satisfies God's desire to set sinners free. Since Jesus received the wrath of God in the place of sinners, there is no wrath left for them, and they can, therefore, go free.

Everyone who has trusted in the redeeming work of Christ can say a hearty 'Amen!' to these words from the apostle Paul: 'There is therefore now no condemnation to those who are in Christ Jesus...' (Rom. 8:1).

But we must also remember that the gospel says the same thing to us that Jesus said to this woman, that is, 'go and sin no more.' The fact that Jesus has paid the price for sinners means that those who believe in him are to break decisively with their sins.

PAUSE TO REFLECT

After telling this woman that he did not condemn her, Jesus spoke these words to those who had gathered around him: 'I am the light of the world. He who follows Me shall not walk in darkness, but have the light of life.'

This is the second of Jesus' seven 'I am' sayings in this Gospel.

TIME OUT

John's Gospel records seven 'I am' sayings from Jesus:

'I am the bread of life' (6:48)
'I am the light of the world' (8:12)
'I am the door' (10:9)
'I am the good shepherd' (10:11)
'I am the resurrection and the life' (11:25)
'I am the way, the truth, and the life' (14:6)
'I am the vine' (15:5)

Jesus' words form a natural conclusion to his conversation with the woman. Having dispelled her darkness, he announces himself as the light of the world.

This saying tells us something about the world that many do not like to hear, namely, it is spiritually and morally dark. Jesus was claiming to dispel this darkness.

The Bible constantly uses darkness as an emblem for man in his natural state. Sinners are described as having hearts (Rom. 1:21) and minds (Eph. 4:18) that are darkened. This is because Satan, who is the prince of darkness and who rules over the kingdom of darkness (Eph. 6:12), has blinded sinners (2 Cor. 4:4).

Every believer in Christ was once in this darkness, but that is no longer the case. A marvellous transformation has taken place. Christians have been called out of darkness into light (1 Peter 2:9) and are now children of light and children of the day (1 Thess. 5:5).

How did this glorious change come about? Through the Lord Jesus! He is the light that dispels the darkness of sin and shines in the hearts of his people (2 Cor. 4:6).

The fact that Jesus is the light of the world cannot be taken to mean that all are automatically freed from the darkness of sin. Jesus only dispels the darkness for those who follow him.

To follow Christ is to commit ourselves wholly and entirely to him as our only hope for forgiveness of our sins and right standing before God.

28.

Two healings for one man

John 9:1-38

The miraculous healing recorded in this chapter took place in the city of Jerusalem, where Jesus and his disciples were attending the Feast of the Tabernacles.

Jesus answers his disciples (vv. 1-5)

When they saw this blind man, Jesus' disciples could only think of two explanations: either the man was being punished for sinning, or his parents had committed a grievous sin.

While all suffering must ultimately be attributed to sin, we must not say that each case of suffering is caused by a specific sin. Sometimes this is true, but it is not true in every case.

Jesus said this man's suffering was not due to a specific sin. It was rather designed by God for a specific purpose — 'that the works of God should be revealed in him' (v. 3).

This man's blindness had been designed for the very moment described in these verses — that moment when Jesus would heal him! Does this constitute something of a 'raw deal'? Not at all. Firstly, this man's story has brought inspiration and comfort to countless numbers. Secondly, this man's physical healing led to his spiritual healing.

Another example of this teaching is found in John 11. There Jesus allowed Lazarus to die so that he, Jesus, could demonstrate his glory by raising him (11:4). It is interesting that Jesus quickly moved from the theological dilemma posed by this man to the work that he, Jesus, had come to do. He points out the urgency of this work ('while it is day' — v. 4). The point we need to see is that there will be an eternity for us to get our questions answered, but this life offers us a very limited time to work for the Lord.

Some may wonder if this verse applies to us in that Jesus was speaking about himself and his work. But the servant is not greater than his master. If the Lord Jesus had work to do, we may rest assured that we do as well.

The things Jesus says here about his approach to his work ought to give pause to all who are his followers. Do we apply ourselves to the tasks he has assigned us with faithfulness? Do we see that our time here is fleeting and that we must work with a sense of urgency? J. C. Ryle says:

> The life that we now live in the flesh is our day. Let us take care that we use it well, for the glory of God and the good of our souls... Our time is very short. Our daylight will soon be gone. Opportunities once lost can never be retrieved.[1]

Jesus heals the blind man (vv. 6-7)

After responding to the disciples' question, Jesus proceeded to make a mudpack, put it on the eyes of the blind man and told him to go and wash in the pool of Siloam.

What was the purpose of the spit and clay? To outward appearances, this combination was offensive and inadequate. But in the hands of Jesus it was effective. In like manner, the cross of Christ appears to be offensive and inadequate in bringing eternal salvation. But in the plan and purpose of God, that cross is effective (1 Cor. 1:18-25).

TIME OUT

What was the purpose of the pool? The word 'Siloam' means 'sent'. It is the same word as 'Shiloh' in Genesis 49:10, which is a prophecy of Christ.

William Hendriksen says the '...deeper meaning is surely this: that for spiritual cleansing one must go to the true Siloam; i.e., to the One who was sent by the Father to save sinners.'[2]

Matthew Henry notes: 'Christ is often called the *sent of God*... so that when Christ sent him to the pool of Siloam he did in effect send him to himself; for Christ is *all in all* to the healing of souls. Christ as a prophet directs us to himself as a priest.'[3]

The man explains his healing (vv. 8-17)

To his acquaintances (vv. 8-12)

The neighbours of the man, who knew him best, confirmed that this was indeed the man they knew, but they wondered how he could now see. Those who previously 'had seen [him]' (v. 8) probably refers to people who had simply passed him on several occasions. They were uncertain about whether the man they were now seeing was the same one that they had seen before.

The curiosity of these people gave the man the opportunity to tell them what had taken place. This he did in simple, straightforward fashion (v. 11).

Every Christian should respond to opportunities to witness for Christ in the same fashion.

To the Pharisees (vv. 13-17)

The Pharisees were outraged by this healing because it was done on the Sabbath. Jesus had performed work by making the mudpack, and the work he had performed was unnecessary (the man could have stayed blind one more day!). While others were divided about Jesus, the healed man was certain that Jesus had made him see (v. 15) and was, therefore, a prophet (v. 17).

Charles Erdman observes:

> The Pharisees were ... in a dilemma; there stood the man; his sight was perfect; he had been born blind; Jesus had opened his eyes. They must either deny the facts or admit the divine nature of Jesus which the facts proved.[4]

We might be inclined to think the healing of a man blind from birth would be the cause of great rejoicing, but it only caused more controversy.

The healed man defends Jesus (vv. 18-34)

The religious leaders used three arguments to get around the evidence for the healing. They first insisted that nothing happened (v. 18).

Desperate to find a way to get around the miracle, the Pharisees met with the man's parents. They were evidently hoping to prove that he had not really been blind at all. Or perhaps they were hoping that the man who claimed to be healed was actually a seeing man who looked like their son.

They may have been hoping that Jesus saw the resemblance, and convinced this man to be 'healed'.

The second argument of the Pharisees was that something had happened but not what the blind man thought (v. 24). They suggested the man had been healed, but not through the power of Jesus. God had done it for him, and Jesus, they argued, just happened to be there fiddling with the mud.

Their third argument was that no one could know for sure what happened (v. 29).

The real problem was that these leaders had drawn their conclusion before looking at the evidence. With that conclusion firmly planted, they would not let the evidence speak for itself but rather looked for a way to get around it. Their strategies are still used against those who claim to have been changed by Christ.

The healed man, refusing to be swayed by the religious leaders, made three truths clear: a dramatic change had taken place (v. 25), that change had taken place at the command of Jesus (vv. 25, 30), the change was of such a nature that it could only be explained as an act of God (v. 33).

Jesus heals the healed man (vv. 35-38)

These verses relate Jesus' second encounter with this man. While the first encounter produced physical healing, this one produced spiritual healing. The man became a believer in Jesus.

We should note that this spiritual healing took place as a result of Jesus seeking this man (v. 35) and revealing the truth to him (v. 37). The man responded to the truth by crying: 'Lord, I believe!' He entrusted himself completely to Jesus as his Saviour and Lord.

PAUSE TO REFLECT

It is obvious that Jesus intended the physical healing of this man to culminate in his spiritual healing. The one was a picture of the other. These healings yield the following conclusions about salvation:

- As this man was physically blind and totally unable to help himself, we are all by nature spiritually blind and helpless (2 Cor. 4:4).

- As this man was physically healed by the grace and power of Jesus, we are spiritually healed by the same means (Eph. 2:8-9).

- As Jesus used seemingly inadequate and absurd means (clay, spit, the pool) to heal this man, he uses his seemingly inadequate and absurd death on the cross to provide salvation (1 Cor. 1:18-25).

- As this man was spiritually healed by believing on Jesus, we are saved in the same way. What does it mean to believe in Jesus? True belief consists of knowing the facts about Jesus, believing those facts are true and trusting in or relying upon those facts for salvation. True belief always involves commitment.

- As this man readily obeyed Jesus' commands (v. 7) and eagerly worshipped him (v. 38), so those who are saved will desire to obey the Lord and to worship Christ.

- As this man encountered opposition because of the change he experienced, so believers in Christ can expect opposition because of the spiritual change he has made in their lives (2 Tim. 3:12).

29.
Three would-be disciples

Luke 9:57-62

The middle portion of Luke's Gospel (9:51 - 19:44) recounts for us the most intriguing journey in all of human history. It tells us of our Lord's final journey to Jerusalem where he was to lay down his life to purchase eternal salvation for all who believe in him.

Most of this long section is taken up with words Jesus spoke. But sprinkled into the accounts of his teaching are several accounts of his encounters with individuals. The rich young ruler, Bartimaeus and Zacchaeus are all here (18:18 - 19:10), as well as others.

The verses above tell us of three men Jesus encountered in quick succession. The key word in these encounters is 'follow'. Two of these men professed their desire to follow Christ (vv. 57, 61), while Jesus issued this command to the other: 'Follow Me' (v. 59).

What does it mean to follow Christ? It means to become his disciple, or, if you prefer, to become a Christian.

The Christian is one who follows Christ. He has stopped following his own way and now follows Christ's way. He has turned from his sins to Christ, received him as Lord and Saviour and now seeks to live according to what he commands. Christ is out front and he, the Christian, is in the rear.

No Christian is a perfect follower of Christ, but, make no mistake about it, every Christian is a follower. The Bible knows nothing of a non-following follower. One might as well speak of a square circle. The Christian may stray from the path of following Christ. He may lag far behind at times. He may even run ahead of his Lord from time to time, but, however imperfectly his following is, he follows.

The issue before us in this passage, then, is that of becoming a child of God, and, tragically, these men all fell short. They teetered on the very verge of genuine discipleship, but failed to finally embrace Christ. They failed because each was in the grip of a peril that waged war on true discipleship.

TIME OUT

Not much has changed since the long-ago day described in these verses. Yes, these men have long since passed off the stage of human history, and the Lord Jesus Christ himself is not now ministering in the flesh as he was then. Yes, we have our computers, our cellular phones, and we can walk on the moon.

But the single greatest issue facing each and every one of us is exactly the same today as it was then. What will we do with the Lord Jesus Christ, the God-man? Will we embrace him as Saviour, follow him, and receive the eternal life he offers? Or will we, as these men did, turn away from him?

What, then, is true discipleship? Of what does it consist?

Those who desire to follow Jesus must put him above personal security and comfort (vv. 57-58)

As Jesus journeys along, the first man draws alongside and says, 'Lord, I will follow You wherever You go' (v. 57).

There was nothing in the man's words to indicate a problem. His profession seems to us to be sincere, and we expect Jesus to welcome him aboard. But Jesus did not. The Gospel accounts frequently remind us that Jesus could read the innermost thoughts of men as easily as we read words on paper (John 2:25; 4:16-19).

While this man was professing his readiness to follow, Jesus was reading him, and what he read there indicated that this man's words were just that: words.

Jesus knew this man had not counted the cost of discipleship, that he would follow him as long as it was convenient and comfortable, but would at the first sign of hardship and difficulty abandon ship.

So Jesus said, 'Foxes have holes and birds of the air have nests, but the Son of Man has nowhere to lay His head' (v. 58). And we read no more of this man. He didn't even follow long enough to encounter hardship. Jesus' words about hardship were enough to make him vanish as quickly as he appeared.

Those who desire to follow Jesus don't delay in committing themselves to the journey (vv. 59-60)

The second man was a procrastinator (vv. 59-60). Perhaps it was as the first man beat a hasty retreat that Jesus turned to this man and said, 'Follow Me.' In other words, Jesus used the failure of the first man to essentially say to this man, 'How about you? Are you ready to follow Me?'

This man may very well have been taken aback by Jesus' blunt command. He may have even stammered and spluttered before he regained his composure. He did not want to follow Jesus, but he knew he had to have a seemingly unanswerable excuse. At last he had it! 'Lord, let me first go and bury my father' (v. 59).

It seems to have been a perfectly legitimate excuse. Here was a man who truly wanted to follow the Lord but had an unavoidable conflict. The Jews considered proper burial as the most important of all duties. It took precedence over the study of the law, the performance of temple service, the killing of the Passover lamb, and the performance of the rite of circumcision.[1]

But wait. Something is not right here. If this man had to bury his father, why was he not doing it? Why was he out here along the road to catch a glimpse of Jesus journeying along? Burials in those days had to be tended to without delay.

The answer is the man's father was not dead yet. The man was, then, asking Jesus to put off his demand for discipleship until his father died and was buried. It was a plea for an indefinite delay. It is obvious that this man had never really seen how vitally urgent and surpassingly important the demands of Christ are.

Jesus saw through this man as easily as he had the first. His words, 'Let the dead bury their own dead...' called him to re-think his priorities and to act decisively and quickly. There was before him a far more pressing and vital matter, namely, his own spiritual life. Those who are spiritually dead can give themselves to tending to the matters of this life. But those who have spiritual life give evidence of it by putting Christ above everything else. After Jesus spoke these words, we read no more of this man. He evidently vanished as quickly as the first.

But his error has not vanished. Many, when confronted with the message of salvation, take up the words of this foolish man: 'Lord, let me first...'

There are many murderers of souls. Doubt about the truth has slain its thousands. Love of ease and comfort has, as well. But I wonder if this business of simply procrastinating will not in the final analysis prove to be the most prolific of all these murderers.

Those who desire to follow Jesus do so willingly and wholeheartedly (vv. 61-62)

The third man presents us with the sad reality of the divided heart (vv. 61-62).

Like the first man, this fellow professed his readiness to follow Jesus, but he quickly added one condition. He must first go to bid farewell to his family.

This also seems to have been a perfectly legitimate request. Jesus had scriptural precedent for granting it. Elijah had allowed Elisha to bid farewell to his family before taking up the work to which Elijah had called him (1 Kings 19:19-21).

But Jesus, that great reader of men, knew the two cases were not equal. Elisha's request came from a heart that was eager to follow, while this man's came from one that was reluctant to follow. To go home and bid farewell was for Elisha the way to show he was making a radical break with his old life and giving himself to his new task. But the man with whom Jesus was dealing made his request from a desire to return home to discuss and deliberate with his family whether he was doing the right thing. He had obviously not yet been seized by the same spirit that gripped Elisha, the spirit that willingly and readily took up God's call.

He was a man who harboured a divided heart. Part of him wanted to follow the Lord, while another part wanted to stay at home.

Many suffer from that same divided heart. They want to be forgiven of their sins and follow Christ, but they also want to hang on to the life of sin.

To all of these, Jesus delivers the same word that he gave to this man. The kingdom of God requires a whole heart. One can no more be saved and hang on to his old life of sin and his love for the world than a farmer can plough a straight furrow by looking in the opposite direction.

PAUSE TO REFLECT

◇◇◇◇◇◇◇◇◇◇◇◇◇◇◇◇◇◇◇◇◇◇◇◇◇◇◇◇◇◇◇◇◇◇◇◇◇

How does the account of these three men find you today? Have you embraced Christ as your Saviour? Are you following him? Or are you repeating one or more of the errors of these men?

Please don't misunderstand the message of these verses. The Lord Jesus is not saying his followers cannot have any possessions or family ties. Other teachings in Scripture make it clear that this is not what Jesus meant at all. What he is teaching is this — the salvation of our souls is of such surpassing and vital importance that nothing, yes, nothing, must be put ahead of it. Personal ease and comfort must be laid aside. The tendency to procrastinate must be laid aside. Love of our old life must be put away. And the Lord Jesus must be trusted and followed. Nothing is more important.

30.
At the home of
◇◇◇◇◇◇◇◇◇◇◇◇◇◇◇◇◇◇◇◇◇◇◇◇◇◇◇◇◇◇◇◇
Mary and Martha
◇◇◇◇◇◇◇◇◇◇◇◇◇◇◇◇◇◇◇◇◇◇◇◇◇◇◇◇◇◇◇◇

Luke 10:38-42

Martha was not wrong to be concerned about preparing food for Jesus and his disciples. It is certainly legitimate when we have guests in our home to be concerned about their comfort and to provide for their needs.

Yet Jesus rebuked Martha. It was a gentle rebuke to be sure. We can almost hear Jesus saying, 'Martha, Martha,' and we realize this is no stern denunciation, but rather a tender rebuke that flowed from genuine concern for Martha herself.

Gentle as it was, it was still a rebuke. And we find ourselves wondering why the rebuke was necessary if Martha was engaged in something that was legitimate.

Some try to get around the problem by taking the words 'one thing is needed' to mean that Martha should have prepared only one dish instead of several. But it is obvious from the next verse that the contrast is not between one dish and several, but rather between what Martha chose, serving in the kitchen, and what Mary chose, listening to Jesus (v. 42).

So we are back to the question of why Jesus would rebuke Martha for doing something that was proper and legitimate.

We can only understand why Martha was wrong when we place her actions alongside Mary's. When Jesus began to speak — and the implication is that he began to teach his disciples — Mary began to listen, while Martha continued bustling about with her preparations. Everything had to be just right, and the more Martha worked to make it so, the more agitated she became. Finally, she reached breaking point, stomped into the presence of Jesus, and demanded that he rebuke Mary for leaving her. By the way, the fact that Mary had 'left' Martha indicates that she, Mary, had been helping but stopped assisting when Jesus began teaching. In all likelihood, more than enough food had already been prepared before Jesus ever arrived (he did, after all, have a habit of giving people advance notice of his visits — Luke 9:52; 10:1; 22:8).

But Martha could not leave it there. She had to go on and on with the preparations until she was exhausted ... and angry! So the spirit in which Martha was going about her work was quite as wrong as the work itself.

TIME OUT

When, then, do legitimate things become wrong? When we put them above spiritual concerns! By continuing to give herself to her work, when the Word of God was being taught, Martha fell into the trap of jumbled priorities. She allowed her concern for the good to crowd out the best. She allowed the constant, mundane part of life to eat up what was unique, tremendously significant and swiftly passing; that is, the opportunity to hear Jesus teach. Jesus had come to provide her with a spiritual feast, but she could not receive it because of her preoccupation with her own feast, a feast of temporal things. She was guilty, therefore, of carrying a legitimate concern to an excessive level, and, in doing so, had failed to take advantage of that which was truly crucial.

If we have a tendency to take Martha's side on this occasion, it could very well be because we all too easily see ourselves in her. If we wince at Jesus' rebuke of her, it could very well be because we know that we deserve it ourselves. The truth is, we all have a tendency to engage in 'Martha' living. We are faced time after time with something that is truly crucial and something that is passing and ephemeral, and time after time we choose the trivial and carry it to excessive levels.

Much of our happiness in this life rests in avoiding the trap of jumbled priorities, in learning what really counts, and living accordingly. It sounds easy, but most of us are finding it to be anything but. We may rest assured that the Spirit of God saw to it that this account was given to us so that we might slip the shackles of 'Martha' living. And we can slip them by keeping in mind three enormously significant principles.

The priority of the Lord

First, the Lord is always to be our priority over everything else. The Lord Jesus allows us no quarter here. When a scribe approached Jesus to ask which is the greatest commandment of all, the Lord Jesus replied in no uncertain terms: '"You shall love the LORD your God with all your heart, with all your soul, and with all your mind." This is the first and great commandment' (Matt. 22:37-38).

Does not your own heart tell you that this is indeed life's supreme priority? Think about it. Your very life is a gift from God. Your health, your family, your friends, your skills, your possessions — all are a gift from almighty God. James was right in saying, 'Every good gift and every perfect gift is from above, and comes down from the Father of lights...' (James 1:17).

In addition to all of these things, the Christian readily confesses that the same God has bestowed upon him the greatest of all gifts, the gift of forgiveness of his sins, and on that basis, this same God will eventually bring him safely into realms of eternal glory.

In the light of all these things, is it not reasonable to say the Lord should be our priority? How few professing Christians actually give him that place! How all of us need to hear the rebuke of the Lord: 'But why do you call Me "Lord, Lord," and not do the things which I say?' (Luke 6:46)!

The importance of the Word of God

Giving priority to the Lord leads, in turn, to a second principle: we cannot give the Lord priority without giving his Word priority. The Lord Jesus does not leave it to us to define for ourselves how we should go about this business of giving him priority. He affirms again and again that it is a matter of consistently taking in his words and allowing them to governing our lives accordingly.

Jesus maintained that his words were so important and vital that one's whole life could be defined in terms of them. His teaching on this point is exceedingly clear. On one occasion, he insisted that the hearing and heeding of his words enables one to be a wise builder who is able to construct a life that is strong and sturdy. Refusing to hear and heed his words makes one a foolish builder who is not able to construct such a life (Matt. 7:24-27; Luke 6:47-49).

He affirmed the priority of his words on another occasion in which another woman had fallen into the trap of jumbled priorities. This woman cried to Jesus from the crowd: 'Blessed is the womb that bore You, and the breasts which nursed You!' Jesus responded by saying, 'More than that, blessed are those who hear the word of God and keep it!' (Luke 11:27-28).

When we come to this matter of the hearing and heeding of the Word of our Lord, we are dealing with a matter that is at the very core of the life of the church. Her worship services are designed to place the Word of God before us. And here is where the account of Martha really hits home. When we have the opportunity to hear the precious word of our Lord, what do we do with it? If we place the fleeting, trivial concerns of this life — no matter how legitimate they may be in and of themselves — above the hearing of the Word of God, we might as well call ourselves 'Martha'!

It doesn't matter whether it comes in the shape of a baseball, basketball, football, or in the form of picnics, fishing lures, movies, concerts, or television shows — when we put it ahead of the Word of God, we have joined Martha in the kitchen.

What, child of God, is the name of your kitchen — that thing, legitimate in its own way, that you use to excuse yourself from hearing and heeding the Word of God?

The lasting good

There is yet another principle suggested by this ancient episode, a principle which may be put in this way: giving priority to the Word of God produces good that can never be taken away.

We must never forget that the Lord Jesus was not just concerned to rebuke Martha but also to commend Mary. In doing the latter, he explicitly said Mary had chosen the 'good part', and he would not take it away from her (v. 42).

A passage of Scripture often contains more than one level of truth. It was certainly so when Caiaphas said it was necessary for Jesus to die so that the whole nation might not perish. He was speaking about the raw political necessity of getting Jesus out of the way, but, unwittingly, he also proclaimed the central truth of the gospel, that it was necessary for Jesus to die so others would not perish (John 11:49-52).

I suggest we can treat the words of Jesus about Mary in the same way. On the surface, they simply mean Jesus was refusing to honour Martha's demand. He would not deprive Mary of the privilege of hearing his words by sending her back to the kitchen. But we do no violence to Scripture if we take those words as a picture of an even greater truth, namely, the words of Christ do good that can never be taken away from those who heed them.

PAUSE TO REFLECT

There is, of course, a great day of 'taking away' for all of us. Practically all the things we hold near and dear in this life are going to finally be taken away from us. Martha's kitchen is going to be closed down. All those things that we have used to excuse ourselves from the Word of God will finally perish, but that very Word that we so often avoided will be left. The prophet Isaiah says, 'The grass withers, the flower fades, but the word of our God stands for ever' (Isa. 40:8).

And on that eternal day those who have paid much heed to the Word of God will be shown to be wise, and those who have not sufficiently heeded it will feel ever so foolish for putting the fleeting, trivial things of this life above that blessed Word. May God help us to live now as we will wish that we had lived on that day.

31.
Ten lepers cleansed

◇◇◇◇◇◇◇◇◇◇◇◇◇◇◇◇◇◇◇◇◇◇◇◇◇◇◇◇◇◇◇◇◇◇◇◇◇◇◇

Luke 17:11-19

Jesus was travelling between Galilee, which was a province of the Jews, while Samaria was, of course, the home of the Samaritans.

Samaritans and Jews did not normally have anything to do with each other. But leprosy was such a terrible disease that it overrode this natural hostility. So we have ten lepers here. Nine were Jews, and one a Samaritan.

TIME OUT
◇◇◇◇◇◇◇◇◇◇◇◇◇◇◇◇◇◇◇◇◇◇◇◇◇◇◇◇◇◇

The *Holman Bible Dictionary* says of leprosy:

A generic term applied to a variety of skin disorders from psoriasis to true leprosy. Its symptoms ranged from white patches on the skin to running sores to the loss of digits on the fingers and toes.

TIME OUT

◇◇◇◇◇◇◇◇◇◇◇◇◇◇◇◇◇◇◇◇◇◇◇◇

For the Hebrews it was a dreaded malady which rendered its victims ceremonially unclean — that is, unfit to worship God (Lev. 13:3). Anyone who came in contact with a leper was also considered unclean. Therefore, lepers were isolated from the rest of the community so that the members of the community could maintain their status as worshippers.[1]

Nationality was one of the few differences among these men. They had much in common. All were lepers. All had heard about Jesus and believed that he could help them. All cried to him for mercy. All obeyed his command to go to the priests. And all were instantaneously healed.

After Jesus healed them, yet another difference emerged. The Samaritan went back to thank Jesus, while the others did not.

This account lays before us some vital truths that we are constantly inclined to forget. We might say that it provides us with four snapshots that we are intended to glue in the album of our minds.

A snapshot of the Lord Jesus Christ

We must not let our interest in these lepers cause us to lose sight of the Lord Jesus. He is the greatest person to ever stride across the stage of human history. He is the theme of the whole Bible. This story joins its voice with those of the other Gospel records to trumpet the truth that Jesus was the God-man.

Think about it! Leprosy was the most dreaded disease of that time, a disease for which there was no cure. But Jesus cured it. Not just in one man, but in ten! And he cured it in all ten with a mere word! Such power! Such grace!

The Lord Jesus is the same today as he was on that occasion. He still abounds in power and grace, and he puts that power and grace on display each and every time that he saves a sinner.

Power and grace? Yes! Every sinner is fast bound in sin. It takes power to break the chains and set him free. And no sinner has any claim on God, any more than those lepers did on Jesus. It is grace that causes Jesus to bestow on sinners what they do not deserve and cannot earn.

A snapshot of human nature

As these men made their way to the priests, they were healed (v. 14). Nine of them, the Jews, continued on their way without so much as a backward glance at Jesus.

It is often said that these men were not thankful. I doubt that. If we could hurl ourselves back through time, find them a couple of days later in the coffee shops of Galilee and ask if they were thankful to Jesus, each one would respond: 'Of course, I am thankful. If it had not been for Jesus, I would still be a leper.'

Why, then, did these men not go back and express their thanks? Perhaps they were at that moment preoccupied with themselves. The thought of being reunited with family members and friends, coupled with the thought of resuming their place in society, crowded out any thought of expressing thanks.

That preoccupation may have combined with something else — the assumption that it is possible to be thankful without expressing it.

A snapshot of thanksgiving

The Samaritan was the only one who returned to give thanks to Jesus. He was the one least likely to do so. Samaritans did not have any use for Jews, but this man returned to Jesus, a Jew, to offer thanks. His thanksgiving was:

- personal — he didn't let someone else do it for him;
- prompt — he didn't wait to do it;
- profuse — he didn't offer it in half-hearted, muted terms.

His gratitude also proved to be productive. Because he went back and thanked Jesus, he received an even greater blessing; that is, the gift of eternal salvation.

His experience leads us to this conclusion: the most thankful are the most blessed.

We want to turn this around. We want to say the most blessed are the most thankful. But it is not true. Many draw deeply from the well of God's blessings without having a truly thankful spirit, and many are genuinely thankful who do not seem to enjoy a great number of blessings.

A snapshot of salvation

I have already indicated that the Samaritan received something the other men did not. They received the temporal blessing of deliverance from leprosy. No small blessing! The Samaritan received the same temporal blessing as well as the spiritual blessing of being delivered from sin (v. 19).

In saving this man, the Lord Jesus reminds us of certain crucial truths:

- We all have a disease that is far worse than leprosy. It is the spiritual disease of sin.

- Jesus alone can cure this disease. He sovereignly and graciously bestows it today, as he did with the Samaritan.

- Not all will be saved.

- Temporal blessings do not signify that we are right with God. Some think so. They say things like this: 'I know I am right with God. I could never have made it this far if I didn't have God in my life.'

PAUSE TO REFLECT

Warren Wiersbe offers this insight:

> Every child of God should cultivate the grace of gratitude. It not only opens the heart to further blessings but glorifies and pleases the Father. An unthankful heart is fertile soil for all kinds of sins (Rom. 1:21ff).[2]

Douglas J. W. Milne adds:

> When people turn to Jesus they show this by thankfulness to God for his salvation. Christ is our principal benefactor to whom we owe all that we are (*1 Cor.* 15:10). Expressed gratitude is a Christian virtue (*Phil.* 4:6; *1 Thess.* 5:18), just as rank ingratitude is the mark of the unbeliever (*Rom.* 1:21)[3] (italics are his).

32.
A poor rich man

Luke 18:18-30

As we have already noted, the middle portion of Luke's Gospel is devoted to the journey of the Lord Jesus Christ to Jerusalem to die on a Roman cross. By that death he would provide eternal salvation for sinners. During the course of his journey, Jesus encountered several intriguing individuals; one of these is known to us as the rich young ruler.

This young man teaches us that it is possible to be right about some important spiritual issues and still miss out on eternal salvation.

What he was right about

The importance of eternal life

As Jesus journeyed along, this young man greeted him with these words: 'Good Teacher, what shall I do to inherit eternal life?' (v. 18).

There can be no doubt about the depth of his interest and the urgency he felt about this issue. Mark's Gospel tells us that he came, not casually strolling to Jesus, but rather running (Mark 10:17). Furthermore, he was so vitally interested that he addressed Jesus in the presence of others (v. 26). He was not embarrassed to let it be known that he wanted to have this most precious of all things, eternal life.

TIME OUT

How different this young man was in comparison to our generation! Most pride themselves on being prepared for every eventuality. They have insurance for their homes, their cars and their bodies. They try to plan ahead for sending their children to college. But while many are very good at preparing for these things, they give no thought at all about preparing for eternity.

The irony is that many of the things for which we diligently prepare are only in the category of things that *might* happen, while eternity is in the category of that which will *definitely* happen. The author of Hebrews says that it is 'appointed' for each of us to die and after this comes judgement (Heb. 9:27).

Coming to Jesus as the authority on eternal life

Jesus is the world's foremost authority on this matter of eternal life. He came to this earth from the realm of eternity (John 3:13), and he came for the express purpose of making it possible for us to enter that eternal realm from which he came. He came to give us eternal life (John 3:16), and there is eternal life in no other (John 3:36; 14:6; Acts 4:12).

What he was wrong about

Thinking Jesus was only a good teacher (v. 18)

Jesus was good and he was a teacher, but accepting him as a good teacher was not enough. Jesus challenged this young man at this point by saying, 'Why do you call Me good? No one is good but One, that is, God' (v. 19).

Jesus was essentially saying, 'Do you really regard me as good in the fullest sense of the word? Are you willing to accept what that implies about me? Do you understand that for me to be really good, I have to be more than a mere man.' In other words, Jesus was declaring himself to be nothing less than God in human flesh.

This young man could not have eternal life if he was not willing to submit to Jesus as God. The young man was right to come to Jesus about eternal life, but he had to recognize that life was not in some sort of formula Jesus would give, but rather in Jesus himself. Many are willing to admit part of the truth about Jesus, but eternal life comes only to those who sincerely acknowledge him as God (1 John 4:15).

Thinking eternal life can be attained through good works

According to Matthew, this young man asked: 'What good thing shall I do that I may have eternal life?' (Matt. 19:16). Jesus answered: '...if you want to enter into life, keep the commandments' (Matt. 19:17).

It seems as if Jesus was agreeing with him, but he was actually showing him how utterly helpless he was in this matter of attaining eternal life. If we could perfectly keep the commandments of God we would be righteous in God's eyes; but no one has ever done so except Christ. If we would be righteous before God, then, we must not look to anything we can do but rather to the righteousness of the Lord Jesus Christ. His righteousness is applied to us when we see how perfectly helpless we are and cast ourselves completely on him.

Turning away from Jesus

After telling him to keep the commandments, Jesus listed five (v. 20). The young man confidently responded: 'All these things I have kept from my youth' (v. 21). If eternal life was a matter of keeping God's commandments, he thought he was well on his way. He couldn't have been more wrong. The Lord Jesus said to him, 'You still lack one thing. Sell all that you have and distribute to the poor, and you will have treasure in heaven; and come, follow Me' (v. 22).

With these words, Jesus brought this young man face to face with the pivotal issue in this business of having eternal life. The rich young man thought he was willing to do anything to secure eternal life. The question was whether he was willing to do the absolutely essential and indispensable thing. Was he willing to break with his idol, material possessions, and submit to Christ and Christ alone? We know how he answered that question. This young man wanted eternal life, but not at the cost of giving up his god. With sorrow he turned away from Christ (v. 23).

PAUSE TO REFLECT

The Lord does not require us to give up all our material possessions to be saved. But he does require that we decisively break with our idols and commit ourselves to him alone as our Lord and Saviour (1 Thess. 1:9).

If your idol is money, the Lord demands that you renounce it and rest solely upon him. If it is pleasure, the Lord demands that you break with it and cast yourself upon him. If it is your own preconceived notions about God and salvation, the Lord demands that you cast them aside and embrace his revealed truth. Even after we are saved, our hearts stray from time to time back to our former gods and our former way of life. But occasional straying is far different from continually serving. No one can be saved who comes to Christ with the intention to keep on serving his idols and following his sins.

When this young man heard Jesus' call to break with his god, his heart sank. He wanted eternal life, but not at the cost of giving up his god. He made his decision. What is your decision? Do you prize eternal life enough to repent of your sins and commit yourself to living under the lordship of Christ? Or will you cling to your sins and turn away from Christ?

33.
Kingship demonstrated

Luke 18:35-43

These verses describe the last leg of Jesus' journey to Jerusalem. We should keep in mind that Jesus had timed his journey to coincide with the Passover celebration. He was, of course, the true Passover Lamb that was to be sacrificed for the sins of the people.

Because it was the Passover season, Jesus was joined on his journey by a great multitude of pilgrims. The Passover always created a great deal of excitement, but this particular year it was running at floodtide. The fame of Jesus had spread throughout the land. On every hand, people were 'buzzing' about whether he was indeed their promised Messiah. So the closer Jesus got to Jerusalem the more the excitement increased. Some thought he was going to Jerusalem to actually claim the throne and set up his kingdom.

While he was passing through Jericho, Jesus encountered two men, Bartimaeus (named in Mark 10:46) and Zacchaeus.

The first encounter demonstrated that he was indeed the Messiah, and further fuelled the euphoria the pilgrims were feeling. The second encounter showed that Jesus was not the kind of Messiah the people were looking for, and temporarily dampened the messianic fervour.

TIME OUT

◇◇◇◇◇◇◇◇◇◇◇◇◇◇◇◇◇◇◇◇◇◇◇◇◇◇

The Jericho of Jesus' time, located south of the Old Testament Jericho that was destroyed by Joshua and the people of Israel (Josh. 6), was, in the words of William Hendriksen, 'a little paradise' with palm trees and rose gardens. Hendriksen adds: 'Herod the Great and his son Archelaus had made it even more beautiful. A grand winter palace had been built there, also a theater and a hippodrome. Some of the streets were lined with sycamore trees. The climate was delightful.'[1]

The plea of Bartimaeus (vv. 35-39)

The plea of a pitiful man

What a pitiful fellow Bartimaeus was! Unable to see, he had been reduced to a life of begging. The account does not tell us how long he had been in this condition, but our sense of things is that it had been for a very long time, perhaps even from birth.

We can well imagine Bartimaeus passing his days with a sense of hopelessness and despair. Then one day a bright ray of hope pierced his gloom. He inquired about the unusually large number of people that were passing by his station and was told that Jesus of Nazareth would soon be coming that way.

He had heard about Jesus. He was the one who had caused the lame to walk, the deaf to hear and, best of all, the blind to see! Perhaps this Jesus who had shown compassion to so many and had healed them of their afflictions would be willing to do the same for him.

So Bartimaeus began to cry out. Again and again, he said, 'Jesus, Son of David, have mercy on me!' (v. 38).

A perceptive plea

Bartimaeus' cry consisted of two parts. First, he called Jesus 'Son of David', which was a messianic title. In using it, Bartimaeus was stating his conviction that Jesus was the one who would fulfil the promises God had made to David, the greatest of Israel's kings. This indicated that Bartimaeus had seriously reflected on what he had heard and became convinced that Jesus was the long-awaited Messiah. God's grace had already been at work in Bartimaeus and had created faith in him.

The second part of Bartimaeus' cry was 'Have mercy on me!' He knew that he had no claim upon Jesus, that there was nothing in him to earn or deserve Jesus' attention. His only hope lay in Jesus caring about his miserable state.

A persistent plea

Some of the multitude took it upon themselves to rebuke Bartimaeus. He was upsetting the decorum of the occasion, he should hush! But Bartimaeus refused to listen. The more he was told to hush, the more he cried out. Again and again he cried: 'Son of David, have mercy on me!' Let those who could see worry about decorum. Bartimaeus would cry! He knew his opportunity was fleeting. Jesus was just 'passing by' (v. 37). There was no time to waste and nothing to lose.

Bartimaeus is a model for those who suffer a far more serious blindness than he — satanically induced spiritual blindness (2 Cor. 4:4) that prevents unbelievers from seeing their sin, the judgement awaiting them and the saving ability of the Lord Jesus Christ. What does Bartimaeus say to these? Your need is great! Jesus is near! His mercy is great! The time is short! Cry! Cry for his mercy!

The kingly response of Jesus (vv. 40-43a)

Jesus was every bit the king on this occasion. In king-like fashion, he 'commanded' that Bartimaeus be brought to him (v. 40). In king-like fashion, he asks the blind man: 'What do you want Me to do for you?' (v. 41).

It seems to be an absurd question. The man was blind! Everyone knew it! Jesus knew it! It was plain that he wanted to receive his sight! Why, then, did Jesus ask? It was not because Jesus was seeking information. It was rather because he wanted Bartimaeus and all those around to understand the connection between God's blessing and honest, humble asking.

The question made it clear that Jesus was poised and ready to meet Bartimaeus' need. It indicated that Jesus had both the willingness and the capacity to help. It was the question of a king who was ready to draw from his vast reservoir of riches to meet the need of a poor subject. All he had to do was ask.

It didn't take Bartimaeus long to seize this golden opportunity. If all Jesus required was asking, Bartimaeus would ask: 'Lord, that I may receive my sight' (v. 41).

In king-like fashion, Jesus grants the request, saying, 'Receive your sight; your faith has made you well' (v. 42).

The happy sequel is recorded in these words: 'And immediately he received his sight, and followed Him, glorifying God. And all the people, when they saw it, gave praise to God' (v. 43).

King Jesus had demonstrated his kingship!

PAUSE TO REFLECT

There is an abundance of mercy with our Lord: mercy for salvation, for the lifting of the burdens of his people and for spiritual renewal of his church. But God has determined that his mercy shall flow to us through the channel of intense desire and bold asking. May God help us to both desire and ask, reminding ourselves as we do of these familiar lines:

> Thou art coming to a king,
> Large petitions with thee bring.
> For His grace and power are such,
> No one can ever ask too much

(John Newton).

34.
Kingship clarified

Luke 19:1-10

How often we look right past the main truth of a passage of Scripture and dwell on something that is incidental!

That tendency often crops up with the story of Zacchaeus. The focus often falls on the fact that he was short of stature and had to climb a tree to see Jesus. But while those details add to the human interest of the story, they are not central. Zacchaeus is not even the main character in this passage. That honour goes to Jesus. He is the one on whom we are to focus. Luke included this incident in his Gospel to help us better understand Jesus.

In particular, the experience of Zacchaeus serves to cast light on the kingship of Jesus and to put it in its proper perspective. False concepts of messiahship abounded in those days, and Jesus often found it necessary to set the record straight. He even told some not to mention the fact that he was the Messiah. This was to prevent further fuelling of false hopes and expectations.

In this passage, however, we find him on his way to Jerusalem to keep his appointment with the cross, and he is now willing to allow the people to talk openly about him as the Messiah. The time had come for him to explicitly affirm his messiahship. That is the reason he did not rebuke Bartimaeus for calling him 'Son of David', a clear messianic title (Luke 18:38).

In his encounter with Zacchaeus, Jesus again demonstrated his kingship, but he also defined it. It was not a political kingdom as the Jews expected. It was rather a spiritual kingdom, and the King himself was to be understood as the seeker and the Saviour of sinners (v. 10).

As we read about Zacchaeus, let's make sure we focus not so much on the little man but rather on the big king, Christ, and his kingdom.

The scope of the Lord's kingdom

Its scope was wide enough that there was room in it even for Zacchaeus, who was a despised tax collector. More than that, he was the head of the tax-collecting bureau in Jericho.

TIME OUT

◇◇◇◇◇◇◇◇◇◇◇◇◇◇◇◇◇◇◇◇◇◇◇◇◇◇◇◇◇◇

The *Holman Bible Dictionary* notes:

> Zacchaeus is called a 'chief among the publicans' (Luke 19:2), probably indicating one who contracted with the government to collect taxes, and who in turn hired others to do the actual work. In New Testament times people bid for the job of chief tax collector and then exacted the tax plus a profit from the citizens. Most of the offices were filled by Romans, although some natives got the bids. Publicans were held in the lowest esteem because of their excessive profits, being placed in the same category as harlots (Matt. 21:32).

So here we have a Jew who was collecting taxes for the Roman government, and was undoubtedly resorting to unscrupulous and ruthless methods to do so. The contempt and disdain the Jewish people and their leaders had for Zacchaeus and his ilk were deep. To them, he was worse than 'scum'. By working for the Romans, he was betraying everything that the Jews held near and dear. If a poll had been taken in Jericho to determine the most disliked people, Zacchaeus would have been at the top of the list, or very near it.

The Jews didn't agree among themselves on many issues of that day, but there was unanimity on one matter — there would be no place in the Messiah's kingdom for Zacchaeus.

We can safely assume that Zacchaeus responded in kind. The more he was hated, the more hateful he became. He saw the hypocrisy of the religious leaders, who preached righteousness but failed to practise it. The more he heard and saw of their 'righteousness', the more hardened he became.

This may very well be the reason that he went to see Jesus, who condemned the mere external righteousness of the Pharisees and proclaimed one of a different kind (Matt. 5:20). Curiosity about this unusual preacher was one thing that compelled Zacchaeus to see him.

On top of that, it would not be at all surprising if Zacchaeus had a gnawing sense of dissatisfaction. While his position had probably made him rich, he felt poor inside. And he also felt dirty and longed to be clean.

The truly remarkable thing is that Jesus stopped at the foot of the tree where Zacchaeus was perched and claimed him. There was room in Jesus' kingdom for Zacchaeus. This was a bombshell!

The Jews thought they were in the Messiah's kingdom by virtue of being Jews. God had, after all, made a covenant with Abraham and they were his descendants. Zacchaeus, on the other hand, had allied himself with the Romans by collecting taxes for them. This meant, in the minds of the Jews, that Zacchaeus had automatically excluded himself from any share in the Messiah's kingdom. By going home with Zacchaeus, Jesus showed that his kingdom must be received by individuals and that no individual is too bad to be saved.

The rising tide of messianic interest slowed for a moment as people grumbled that Jesus was going to be the guest of Zacchaeus (v. 7). This was not the kind of king they had in mind!

The qualities of the king

His knowledge

Flashing through Jesus' dealings with Zacchaeus was irrefutable evidence that he was indeed the Messiah. First, there was his penetrating knowledge. Jesus called Zacchaeus by name, and there is no indication that anyone had mentioned his name.

This is not the first time that Jesus had called a name without being informed of it. Nathanael was astounded that Jesus knew his name. How could such a thing be? Jesus answered: 'Before Philip called you, when you were under the fig tree, I saw you.'

There was only one thing Nathanael could say to knowledge like that: 'Rabbi, You are the Son of God! You are the King of Israel!' (John 1:47-49).

That same response would have been fitting for all who heard Jesus call Zacchaeus by name. They were in the presence of divine knowledge, but they missed the enormity of the moment.

His authority

Jesus spoke to Zacchaeus as we would expect a king to speak to one of his subjects — with authority! Jesus took the initiative with him. He did not wait for Zacchaeus to invite him. S. G.

DeGraaf writes: 'Like a king, the Lord Jesus laid claim to Zaccheus and his house.'[1]

Everyone who comes to the Lord Jesus responds to divine initiative. All come in response to his kingly command. Jesus himself affirmed this in these words: 'No one can come to Me unless the Father who sent Me draws him...' (John 6:44).

Jesus is ever the seeker and the Saviour (v. 10) of sinners.

His life-changing power

Jesus' actions had a profound effect on Zacchaeus, who announced his intention to restore four times as much as he had fraudently taken. This was much more than the law required (the original amount plus one fifth — Lev. 6:5; Num. 5:7).

Zacchaeus also promised to give half of his possessions to the poor. It is interesting that Zacchaeus changed immediately. 'I give' (v. 8) is in the present tense. Zacchaeus didn't promise to begin living for the Lord. He started the very moment he received Christ.

How are we to explain such a dramatic change? Zacchaeus was in the hands of the one who changes human hearts!

PAUSE TO REFLECT

We may be inclined to look down our noses at Zacchaeus for being such a low-life fraud, but the truth is that he lives in each of us. We all operate in Zacchaeus-like fashion — thinking about ourselves and ignoring the righteous demands of God and the needs of our neighbours.

The piercing question is this: how can the change we so profoundly need become a reality? We cannot legislate, regulate or educate ourselves into it. People cannot be truly changed until they meet the life-changing king that Zacchaeus met.

The thrilling news is that we can meet him. That same Jesus went from his appointment with Zacchaeus to his appointment with the cross. After he died there, he arose from the grave. He lives today, and he saves today. The author of Hebrews puts it perfectly: 'Therefore He is also able to save to the uttermost those who come to God through Him, since He always lives to make intercession for them' (Heb. 7:25).

The change we all need is available in Jesus Christ. The most urgent business before us is to 'make haste and come' to Jesus (v. 5).

35.

An astonishing proof of an
astonishing claim

John 11:17-44

Most people reject the Christian faith. We can go further. They not only reject, but they are very secure and sure in their rejection of it. The claims of Christianity seem to make no impression upon them at all.

So why do we continue in this way? Why do we continue to hold the Christian faith in a world that has largely abandoned it? What is the point of it all?

We could give many answers to that question, but there is one answer in particular: we cannot get away from the truth about Jesus! Prove to us that Jesus was not God in human flesh, that he was just another man, and we will have to abandon our faith.

Proving Jesus to be just another man is no small task. He is the stubborn, inescapable Christ!

The passage before us gives shining and sparkling evidence that Jesus was no mere man.

We could point to all kinds of proofs, but no single episode in the life and ministry of Jesus more powerfully shows him to be the God-man than his raising of the dead Lazarus. Here is an event of a most striking nature that was performed in the presence of many witnesses. We cannot ignore it or its implications. Jesus made the astonishing claim that he was God. Here he gives us an astonishing proof of that astonishing claim.

Let's divide our consideration of this glorious event into three parts.

The awful tyranny of death (vv. 17-24)

Three words seem to summarize what Jesus found when he got to Bethany.

Hopelessness

The hopelessness is forcefully brought home by one phrase — 'he had already been in the tomb four days' (v. 17).

The Jews held to the notion that the human spirit hovered around the body for three days to see if it was going to come back to life and could be re-inhabited. On the fourth day, the spirit completely left the body, and, as far as the Jews were concerned, the situation was irretrievable or irreversible.

Helplessness

The helplessness of the situation comes out in verse 19. There we are told the Jews gathered around Mary and Martha 'to comfort them concerning their brother'.

Here is utter helplessness in the face of death. The Jews could do nothing about the dead. All they could do was to give as much aid as possible to the living.

Bewilderment

The bewilderment Jesus found is expressed by Martha in verses 20-24. It is apparent from these verses that the darkness of grief and the light of hope were locked in deadly combat in her heart. At one moment she expresses despair. The next moment she expresses optimism.

On one hand, she knew Jesus could have prevented Lazarus from dying and she wonders why he didn't come. The next moment she is taking consolation from the fact that her brother would ultimately rise from the dead. Every believer who has ever had death invade his circle of family or friends has all the commentary he needs on what Martha was going through.

The awesome authority of Jesus over death (vv. 25-44)

He claimed this authority (vv. 25-37)

Death reigns like a tyrant over the human race. A reign is composed of an inauguration and an administration. Death was inaugurated when sin came into the human race.

Since its inauguration death has carried on a threefold administration:

- physical death — the soul is separated from the body;
- spiritual death — the soul is separated from God;
- eternal death — body and soul are separated from God for ever.

In claiming to be the resurrection and the life Jesus was claiming authority over each of these manifestations of death. He pulls the sting of physical death, by promising to raise the body from the grave (v. 25).

He reverses spiritual death by granting spiritual life ('whoever ... lives in Me' — v. 26). He guarantees that those who know him as Lord and Saviour will never die eternally (v. 26).

It must be noted that these great promises have a condition attached to them. They apply only to those who believe in Jesus. Martha believed. May God help us to do so as well.

Yet if Jesus has authority over death, why did he weep at the grave of Lazarus? Why did he weep and feel troubled when he knew that Lazarus would soon be standing beside him in hale and hearty condition?

The word 'groaned' (v. 33) comes from a Greek word, which depicts a stallion rearing, pawing the air and snorting. The word 'troubled' (v. 33) comes from a Greek word which means 'to stir up'. The word 'wept' (v. 35) translates a word which means 'shed tears'. It is not the same weeping as we find in verses 31 and 33, which involved loud expressions of grief.

Jesus' weeping was due, then, to the utter revulsion he felt towards the ugliness of sin and the damage it creates.

TIME OUT

Os Guinness says of Jesus:

> He was moved deeply in the sense of a furious inner anger. Entering His Father's world as the Son of God, He found not order, beauty, harmony, and fulfillment, but fractured disorder, raw ugliness, complete disarray — everywhere the abortion of God's original plan.[1]

Guinness further says that Jesus was sorrowing over

> ...the awesome dichotomy between what God made and meant man to be and what man had made and marred the situation into being.[2]

Jesus' sorrow should make us ask if we feel any outrage, any indignation, as we walk through this world. If we are like him, we must. How sad it is that so many of his people often seem to feel at home in this dark, perverted world!

We must also take note that while Jesus was angry at sin, he was not angry at himself. This indicates that God is not responsible for sin and all the heartache it causes.

He demonstrated this authority (vv. 41-44)

His communion with the Father (vv. 41-42). After reassuring Martha, Jesus spoke to the Father. If Jesus found it necessary to pray, how much more should we! His words were spoken loudly enough (v. 42) to let those around him know that what he was about to do was in conjunction with God and in complete dependence on him. In other words, Jesus framed his action in terms of the issue between himself and the religious leaders, namely, whether he was equal with God.

His command to Lazarus (vv. 43-44). The Greek word for 'cried' is used only here in connection with the Lord, and it signifies a very loud, piercing cry. Our Lord obviously intended for all those around to know exactly what was taking place.

The greatness of the Lord's power is brought out in two ways. First, it revived Lazarus. As powerful as death is, it was unable to retain Lazarus in its grip.

Second, it carried Lazarus out of the tomb. We usually picture Lazarus walking out of the tomb in response to Jesus' cry, but the fact that he was still 'bound hand and foot' when he came out indicates that he was carried out of the tomb by the power of the Lord Jesus.

In relating this miracle, the Holy Spirit refused to supply answers to many of our questions. Where was Lazarus' soul while his body was in the grave? Was it not unkindness to bring him back? Did Lazarus know where his soul had been and could he give an account of it? We must assume that such questions are not answered because God wants us to concentrate on the power and glory that the Lord Jesus demonstrated in raising Lazarus.

PAUSE TO REFLECT

Jesus divided men in everything he said and did. One would think there could be no division after such a grand display, that all would be forced to admit Jesus was nothing less than God in human flesh and would have to bow before him in submission and faith. Some did (v. 45). But others were so hard in their hearts that this event only caused them to be more intense in their hatred of Jesus and more determined to eliminate him (v. 53).

We shouldn't be surprised at this because we still see the very same thing today. Jesus still divides men into the same two camps of believers and unbelievers.

36.
A loving act from a loving heart

John 12:1-8

The anointing of Jesus by Mary occurred at Bethany at the house of Simon the leper (Matt. 26:6). Having been healed, we presume, by Jesus, Simon chose this way to honour him. He also invited Mary, Martha and Lazarus. Since Jesus had raised Lazarus from the dead a few days earlier, Lazarus and his sisters would have welcomed the opportunity to share in honouring Jesus. In fact, it appears that Lazarus also was an honoured guest (v. 2).

Martha, of course, was busy serving (v. 2), but apparently without the anxiety and distraction of a former time (Luke 10:38-42).

Mary was again at Jesus' feet. G. Campbell Morgan says, 'She sat at His feet, when the sun was shining. Then when the darkness was round about her, and Lazarus was dead, and her heart was breaking, she came when He sent for her, and went straight to His feet. Now it was His day of approaching sorrow, and again she went straight to His feet.'[1]

This time, however, Mary was at his feet, not only to listen but also to give concrete expression of her love for him. She took a pound of very expensive ointment and anointed his head (Matt. 26:7) and his feet. She then loosed the long tresses of her hair and proceeded to use them to dry the feet of Jesus. Judas and some of the others (Matt. 26:8) protested vigorously at this 'waste', but Jesus defended it.

Such a lavish, uninhibited expression of love deserves closer scrutiny, for, the truth is, very few of us love Christ as we should, and it's urgent that we begin to do so. Therefore, let's try to go back through time and put ourselves there with Jesus, Mary and the others.

What prompted this expression of love

Two strong factors combined in Mary's heart and drove her to this expression of love.

Gratitude

The more obvious of the two was her gratitude for what Jesus had done for her and her family. Mary had so much for which to thank Jesus. He had visited their home on more than one occasion. He had instructed them in the things of God. When Lazarus died, Jesus spoke words of comfort and hope (11:25-26) and proceeded to raise him from the dead. All of these things and more must have gone racing through her mind as she sat there watching Jesus and Lazarus, and listening to them talk and laugh. Overwhelmed with the realization of what she owed Jesus, Mary slipped away, took the prized ointment, and returned to anoint Jesus.

Understanding

Mary's act was also prompted by understanding. She had procured this ointment especially for the time of Jesus' burial. That is the only logical explanation for Jesus' words: '...she has kept this for the day of My burial' (v. 7).

On this night she evidently realized his death was near. Morgan suggests that she looked into his eyes and 'saw the sorrow there'[2]

She must also have realized that there was a strong possibility that his enemies would not allow his body to be anointed. She concluded, then, that there would never be another opportunity better than the one at this time.

Jesus had often predicted his death at the hand of his enemies (Matt. 16:21; Mark 8:31-32; 9:12; 10:32-34; John 6:52-56; 7:33; 8:21-23), but only Mary seemed to really understand, prompting William Hendriksen to remark: 'Mary was, perhaps, the best listener Jesus ever had.'[3]

If Mary felt such gratitude, shouldn't we? Has Christ done any less for those of us who are saved than he did for her? No, we have not had any family members raised from the dead, but all who know Christ have had their dead souls quickened (Eph. 2:1-7); and in due time we shall have all our brothers and sisters in Christ raised from the dead (1 Thess. 4:13-18)!

If Mary had such an understanding of Christ, shouldn't we? She came to her understanding without the benefit of a complete disclosure of the necessity and meaning of Jesus' death. We, on the other hand, have in the Bible everything we need to know about Jesus' death. We can read about the cross being the very wisdom and power of God (1 Cor. 1:18-25). What Mary saw faintly, we can see clearly.

If we feel gratitude to Jesus as Mary did, and if we understand Jesus even better than she did, why do we not show the same sacrificial, self-forgetful love she did? That is the burning question! The main issue before our churches today is whether we have a passionate love for Christ.

So Mary's expression of love was prompted by gratitude and understanding.

What this expression of love prompted

It did not take long for Mary's action to create a reaction! Acts of love for Christ seldom go undetected or unchallenged. Mary's action set off a wave of criticism. Judas professed to be indignant over such unscrupulous waste. He took this opportunity to portray himself as a champion of the downtrodden (vv. 4-5). John tells us that Judas was not as great a champion of the poor as he pretended to be: 'This he said, not that he cared for the poor, but because he was a thief, and had the money box; and he used to take what was put in it' (v. 6). At that time, however, the other disciples were unaware of what a sinister rascal he was, and they were persuaded by his 'humanitarian' appeal (Matt. 26:8; Mark 14:4-5). So Mary had to contend with not one, but several critics. The apostle Paul says love 'bears all things' and 'endures all things' (1 Cor. 13:7). Mary's love certainly had a lot to bear and endure!

Yet over against the sting of criticism came a soothing commendation from the Lord himself. How often he grieved over the ignorance, faithlessness and lovelessness of his disciples. But here was a disciple who really understood and who loved without limits. When the critics spoke up, Jesus immediately came to her defence. All who love the Lord as fully as Mary may rest assured that he delights in defending them also from satanic attack.

Surely the Lord must be grieved today that so few of us express our love without reservation. I fear many of us are Laodicean Christians. We have become lukewarm in our affection to Christ (Rev. 3:14-22). How refreshing it would be to our Lord, if he could but see a re-kindling of our first love.

Mary's act also had to have a profound impact on the disciples. First, it taught them the urgency of love. It forced them to evaluate their priorities. Jesus said, 'For the poor you have with you always, but Me you do not have always' (v. 8).

Can you imagine how those words, 'Me you do not have always', returned time after time to awaken these disciples with a start, to haunt their minds and to stab their consciences? Even these poignant words didn't have immediate effect upon them, for a few nights later they slept while Jesus prayed in agony. We are so slow to learn the lesson Mary teaches — to love while we can.

TIME OUT

Thomas Carlyle had neglected his wife over the years. One day she was suddenly snatched from him. Only then did Carlyle realize what he had so long taken for granted. Hear the solemn words of Carlyle:

> Cherish what is dearest while you have it near you, and wait not till it is far away. Blind and deaf that we are, O think, if thou yet love anybody living, wait not till death sweep down the paltry little dust clouds and dissonances of the moment, and all be made at last so mournfully clear and beautiful, when it is too late.[4]

Jesus wasn't calling his disciples to neglect the poor, but rather to a sensitivity of the preciousness of that moment. He was urging them not to let the good — feeding of the poor — become the enemy of the best — loving and worshipping him.

They were in danger of subjecting the unique and urgent to the usual and constant. Matthew Henry writes:

> That good duty which may be done at any time ought to give way to that which cannot be done but just now.[5]

Such is the urgency of love. But Mary's act also taught them the fervency of love. Mary allowed her heart to speak freely in this act. We are so prone to temper our love, to be half-hearted in it. The major hindrance to the cause of Christ in our day is the half-hearted love of his disciples. If we would learn from Mary to love fervently without hesitation or reservation, the kingdom of our Lord would advance with mind-boggling success!

PAUSE TO REFLECT

G. Campbell Morgan declares:

> I would rather be in succession to Mary of Bethany than to the whole crowd of the apostles.[6]

37.

A celebrating crowd

and a crying king

Luke 19:28-44

Jesus' arrival in Jerusalem marks the beginning of what has come to be known as 'Holy Week'. This week, which began with Jesus being hailed and acclaimed as King of the Jews, ended with him dying in shame and agony on a Roman cross.

TIME OUT

The last week of Jesus can be summarized as follows:

Sunday:	The triumphant entry into Jerusalem
Monday:	The day of symbolic actions (cursing the fig tree, cleansing the temple)
Tuesday:	The day of controversy (with chief priests, scribes, elders, Pharisees, Herodians and Sadducees)
Wednesday:	The day of silence

TIME OUT

Thursday:	The Passover feast, ministry to the disciples, prayer in the garden, betrayal and arrest
Friday:	The trials before the Sanhedrin and Pilate, crucifixion and burial
Saturday:	The Sabbath
Sunday:	The resurrection

Perhaps no single week in history produced a greater change. On Sunday the people were waving their palm branches and crying, 'Hosanna!' On Friday they were shaking their fists and crying, 'Crucify Him!'

None of this caught Jesus by surprise. He offered a kind of kingdom that people weren't interested in, and he knew that when the people realized this they would reject him.

Excitement had been building for a period of several days about Jesus. As far as many were concerned, his recent raising of Lazarus from the dead proved that he was indeed their long-awaited Messiah. These people were also convinced that the Passover season was right for Jesus to claim his throne. What better time could there be for deliverance from Rome than the celebration of their fathers' deliverance from Egypt?

Such thinking led some to closely monitor every move Jesus made. Early on this particular Sunday morning, they went to nearby Bethany (about two miles away — John 11:18) where Jesus had been staying.

The celebrating crowd (vv. 28-40)

Jesus knew the mood of the swarming multitude. He knew they were ready to acclaim him as King. All they were waiting for was a definite signal from him.

A celebrating crowd and a crying king

Jesus gave that signal by issuing crisp commands to his disciples. Go find a colt. Loose it. Bring it. If anyone were to ask what they were doing, they were to respond: 'Because the Lord has need of it' (Luke 19:31). This is, by the way, the only time in the Gospels in which Jesus refers to himself as Lord.

The colt, on which no one had ever ridden, seems to recognize its Creator and offers no resistance, and Jesus begins to make his way to the city of Jerusalem.

Having taken notice of these preparations, some assumed Jesus was about to 'make his move'. They ran to the city of Jerusalem to spread the news. A large throng made their way from the city toward Bethany. Meanwhile, another large throng accompanied him from Bethany.

Somewhere between Bethany and Jerusalem the two throngs merged. A glorious, intoxicating euphoria reigned, as the people waved the branches they had chopped off the palm trees lining the road and shouted, 'Hosanna' ('Save now!'). Jerusalem had never seen anything to match it.

We should note that Jesus willingly accepted the acclamation of this multitude. On previous occasions he had instructed people not to say that he was the Messiah. But here he offers no objection to the surging throng crying:

> '"Blessed is the King who comes in the name of the LORD!"
> Peace in heaven and glory in the highest!'
>
> (Luke 19:38).

And when the Pharisees demanded that he rebuke the people, Jesus simply responded: 'I tell you that if these should keep silent, the stones would immediately cry out' (Luke 19:40).

What is going on here? Jesus was forcing the hand of the religious leaders. In his Gospel, John writes: 'The Pharisees therefore said among themselves, "You see that you are accomplishing nothing. Look, the world has gone after Him!"' (John 12:19).

This is a statement of sheer terror on the part of the Pharisees. Yes, they wanted to kill Jesus (John 11:53), but it is certain that they did not want to do it during the Passover while Jerusalem was swelled with pilgrims.

After the Passover, when things were back to normal, when it could be done quietly — that was the time to kill Jesus.

Yet the Pharisees' timetable was not God's. His Son must not only die on the cross, he must also die at exactly the right time. He had to die during the Passover as the Lamb of God represented by the original Passover under Moses.

By creating the tremendous atmosphere of excitement and by carefully orchestrating his entrance into Jerusalem, the Lord Jesus Christ was doing nothing less than forcing the religious leaders to accept his and the Father's timetable.

The triumphal entry was a ringing affirmation of Jesus' intention to go to the cross at precisely the time the Father had ordained.

The crying king (vv. 41-44)

All would seem to be well. Here is an acknowledgement of Jesus as the King of the Jews. They appear to have finally come to their senses and are now accepting him. What could possibly be wrong with this?

But there *was* something wrong. Luke's Gospel indicates this by telling us that Jesus wept as he approached the city.

What was there for Jesus to weep about, if this was a true acceptance of him? The answer is, of course, that there would have been nothing for him to weep about if this had been true acceptance, but it was not.

The people were hailing him, not for the king he came to be, but rather for the king they wanted him to be. In other words, they were hailing or acknowledging him as a temporal, political

Messiah who was about to overthrow the Romans and lead Israel back to a position of supremacy among the nations.

They did not realize that Jesus had not come to save his people from the Romans, but rather to save them from something far worse — their sins!

The multitude was so caught up in the euphoria of the moment that the obvious symbolism that Jesus had chosen was lost on them. The Messiah they wanted should have been mounted on an impressive stallion, but Jesus came riding on a lowly donkey. He was clearly demonstrating the nature of his kingship. It was not one that was set up by political force.

If the multitude had realized this, they would have said, 'This is not our Messiah!' and thrown down their palm branches at once. But they had misread their own Scriptures. The prophet Zechariah made it clear that this was their Messiah (Zech. 9:9). But when it became obvious that Jesus was not the Messiah they expected him to be, they consented to his crucifixion.

PAUSE TO REFLECT

Many today are guilty of repeating the error of the multitude. They acknowledge Christ, but it is the acknowledgment of the Christ they want him to be, rather than the Christ he is.

They are only interested in a Jesus who helps them with the problems and challenges of life. They want one who offers them happiness here and now — one who makes life a little smoother and easier.

The sad fact is that multitudes today are very much like Esau of old — willing to barter away that which is of lasting value in order to secure comfort and ease for the moment (Gen. 25:29-34).

Talk to them about eternity, and they are not interested. But talk to them about a Jesus who gives them health and wealth, and they start waving their palm branches!

How is it with you? Have you accepted the Christ who died on the cross to save sinners from eternal doom as your Christ? Or have you set him aside so that you can construct a Christ who suits you and hail him?

Be assured of this — no matter how many Christs you choose to construct, there is only one true Christ, and that is the Christ of the cross. We may receive him to the salvation of our souls or reject him to the immense loss of our bodies and souls in eternal destruction (2 Thess. 1:8-10).

38.

Jesus washes the disciples' feet

◇◇

John 13

Chapters 13 to 19 of John's Gospel describe events that took place in less than twenty-four hours and ended with Jesus being crucified and buried. The disciples were not aware of what lay ahead, but Jesus could see it all down to the last detail. He must have looked forward with eager anticipation to sharing this last supper with the disciples. It would be the last bit of peace before the storm broke!

Jesus stoops (vv. 1-5)

Why did Jesus wash the disciples' feet? Their feet were dirty! The streets and roads of that day were so dusty that the feet became contaminated by walking a short distance. It was customary, therefore, for a host to provide for the rinsing of the feet when guests arrived. This was normally the job of one of the household servants.

Jesus and his disciples apparently rented this room for their supper with the understanding that there would be no host or servant there. Therefore, the owner of the room only provided the water, the basin and the towel. In such a case, the task of washing the feet of the guests fell to the lowest person. But no disciple was willing to admit that he was beneath the others. As a matter of fact, they would argue that very evening about 'which of them should be considered the greatest' (Luke 22:24). It is not surprising, then, that they all walked right past the water and the basin and took their places at the table.

They must have been shocked at what happened next. Jesus suddenly rose from his place and began the menial task. The greatest among them was willing to do the work of the lowest!

TIME OUT

The disciples of Jesus would eventually understand that Jesus, in washing their feet, had provided them with a picture of his work of redemption, in which he rose from his throne, laid aside his glory, girded himself with humanity, poured out his blood, cleansed his people from their sin and returned to glory to sit down at the right hand of God.

Simon Peter objects (vv. 6,8)

We can picture Simon Peter watching carefully as Jesus made his way from one disciple to the other. He, Simon, could not believe that James, John, Thomas and the others would allow Jesus to wash their feet! Why could they not see that this was not right? Why could Jesus not see that this was beneath his dignity?

As Simon watched, he formulated a plan. When Jesus came to him, he, Simon, would set things right! When Jesus reached him, Simon asked: 'Lord, are You washing my feet?' (v. 6).

It was not appropriate for their Master to be washing the feet of his servants, and Simon would point this out! We can also picture him drawing his feet up under him up as he says to Jesus, 'You shall never wash my feet!' (v. 8).

The same disciple who could so easily see the 'inappropriateness' of Jesus washing feet failed to see the inappropriateness of a disciple rebuking his master!

Jesus answers (vv. 7-11)

Simon must have been surprised by Jesus' answer: 'If I do not wash you, you have no part with Me' (v. 8).

What was Jesus saying? If Peter could not accept Jesus humiliating himself to wash the disciples' feet, he, Peter, would not be able to share in that redemption that would only be provided through complete humiliation on the cross. R. V. G. Tasker says that in making his protest, Peter was unwittingly 'displaying the pride of unredeemed men and women, who are so confident of their ability to save themselves that they instinctively resist the suggestion that they need divine cleansing. They desire to do everything for themselves.'[1]

Peter, not wanting to be cut off from Christ, went to the opposite extreme by asking Jesus to give him a bath. But Jesus pointed out that he only needed his feet washed. Peter undoubtedly did not understand until later what Jesus was saying. The Christian gets a once-for-all bath when he is saved. After that, he never again needs a bath, but he does need to have his feet cleansed on a daily basis. Although the Christian is saved for ever, he still gets contaminated by sin as he walks through this world. He does not need to be saved again, but he does need to confess and be cleansed of those sins he commits.

Jesus applies (vv. 12-17)

If the one they called 'Lord' and 'Master' had been willing to stoop in menial service, the disciples should be willing to serve others. Some have taken these verses to mean that churches should conduct foot-washing, but that misses the point. Jesus washed the disciples' feet to meet a real need. Their feet were dirty. We do not follow his example by meeting in our churches to wash feet that are already clean, but rather by helping our brothers and sisters in Christ with their needs. We need to remember that it is much easier to wash clean feet in a service where others are watching than it is to meet real needs when no one is watching.

PAUSE TO REFLECT

James Montgomery Boice concludes from Jesus' words of application:

> What Jesus is talking about is humility and the need for God's people to take a servant role. He is simply saying, 'If I, your Master, have played the servant role, you who are My servants should certainly play the servant role with one another.' We are to care for those who can no longer care for themselves — our aged parents, the poor, orphans. We are to get close to those who are suffering and do everything in our power to alleviate their suffering. We are to open our homes to the lonely. Above all, we are not to take the first place in Christian gatherings but are to take a lower place that someone else might be honoured.[2]

39.

One meal ended, another begun

<<<<<<<<<<<<<<<<<<<<<<<<<<<<<<<<<<<<<<<<<<<<<<<<<<<<<<<<<<<<<<<<<<

Luke 22:14-22

After washing the disciples' feet, Jesus observed the Passover feast with them. This was to be a Passover feast like no other. It was to be their last. Midway through the feast, the Lord Jesus put something new in its place: the Lord's Supper.

This transition was perfectly fitting. The Passover, designed to commemorate the deliverance of the people of Israel from political bondage in Egypt, always had in view the far greater deliverance that Jesus would achieve for his people: deliverance from bondage to sin and Satan. Now that Jesus was about to accomplish that deliverance on the cross, it was only appropriate that the Passover should give way to the Lord's Supper. William Hendriksen observes of the Passover:

> A few more hours and the old symbol ... will have served
> its purpose forever, having reached its fulfillment in the
> blood shed on Calvary... Nevertheless, by historically
> linking Passover and the Lord's Supper so closely together

Jesus also made clear that what was essential in the first was not lost in the second. Both point to *him*, the only and all-sufficient sacrifice for the sins of his people. Passover pointed forward to this; the Lord's Supper points back to it.[1] (italics are his)

TIME OUT

◇◇◇◇◇◇◇◇◇◇◇◇◇◇◇◇◇◇◇◇◇◇◇◇◇◇◇

There has been much debate as to whether the Last Supper actually coincided with the Passover. The Gospel of John says the supper took place before the Passover (John 13:1), while the other Gospels affirm that it was during the Passover (Luke 22:7).

There is no real contradiction. Some minority groups in Jerusalem used a different calendar and celebrated the Passover early. Jesus and his disciples probably followed this unofficial calendar. This made it possible for Jesus to observe the Passover with his disciples, as Matthew, Mark and Luke have it, and die the next day on the Passover, as John has it.

The opening statement (vv. 15-16)

Jesus began his observance of the Passover by sharing with his disciples the deep emotion he felt on this occasion. That ocean of emotion was fed by streams. The first was his love for his disciples, with whom he shared this Passover. There is no small delight in those words 'with you' (v. 15).

The love Jesus had for those men extends to his disciples of all ages. How do we know this? When he died on the cross the next day, it was not just for those disciples with him in the Upper Room, but rather for all those whom the Father had given him.

His impending death was a second stream that fed Jesus' emotion. The cross toward which he had steadily moved from eternity past — that cross by which he would purchase eternal salvation for all his people — was now right before him. How could he not be filled with emotion now that the finish line was so clearly in view?

His emotion was also due to his anticipation of the future glory he would share with his people. He tells his disciples that he will never again eat of the Passover feast 'until it is fulfilled in the kingdom of God' (v. 16). William Hendriksen restates the words of Jesus and then explains them:

> 'I shall never eat of it again until its typical and symbolical meaning has become fully realized in the new heaven and earth.' It is there that the deliverance of his people, not from Egypt, but from all sin and evil will have been fully accomplished. It is there that they will at last have been fully redeemed. It is there also that the fellowship between himself and all the redeemed will have been perfected...[2]

The first cup (vv. 17-18)

Having made his opening statement, the Lord proceeded to bless the cup and pass it to his disciples. As the cup went from disciple to disciple, Jesus essentially pointed them again to the glorious future awaiting them. Yes, his fellowship with them here would soon come to an end, but only to be renewed in eternity, where it would never be interrupted or broken again.

The bread (v. 19)

The blessing and passing of the bread is the point at which Jesus made the transition from the Passover to the Lord's Supper. The unleavened bread of the Passover is now given new significance. From this point forward, the disciples are to associate it with his body. They were to eat this bread in the future as a commemoration of him giving up his body in death for them.

The second cup (v. 20)

After the disciples had eaten of the bread, the Lord Jesus passed another cup to them, saying, 'This cup is the new covenant in My blood, which is shed for you.'

As the bread was intended to commemorate him giving his body, so the cup was designed to commemorate the shedding of his blood for his people. Jesus emphatically connects the shedding of his blood with the establishment of a new covenant.

The fact that all the saints of the Old Testament era were saved from their sins by looking forward in faith to Christ compels us to ask what is now new.

It is not that there is a new plan of salvation. As noted, the people of the Old Testament were saved by the redeeming work of Christ. God has always had only one plan of salvation! That is the reason Jesus is called 'the Lamb slain from the foundation of the world' (Rev. 13:8).

The newness lies in the taking of the blessings of the old to a whole new level. It lies in truth being more clearly revealed, more fully enjoyed and more widely embraced (including Gentiles). It lies in moving from the law of Moses, which showed the awesome holiness of God, his demand for perfect righteousness and the radical sinfulness that precludes us from achieving that righteousness, to Jesus' gracious fulfilment of that law on behalf of believing sinners (John 1:17).

These are privileges purchased for us by the Lord Jesus pouring out his blood on the cross. Let us be absolutely clear that there is no agreement or friendship with God apart from that. Sin is ever the great impediment to our fellowship with God, and there is only one way that sin can be taken out of the way: its penalty has to be paid, either by the sinner himself or by someone on his behalf.

In all of history, there has only been one person who could pay for the sins of others. Jesus! I cannot pay for anyone else, because I have my own for which to pay. Having no sins of his own, Jesus could stand in the place of others. How could one person pay for the sins of many? Because he was God in human flesh, he was an infinite person. He could, therefore, pay for more than one.

On the day after instituting this supper, the sinless Jesus went to the cross to pay for the sins of others. There he poured out his blood. There he endured the wrath of God in the stead of sinners so that all who believe in him will never have to endure that wrath themselves. And this is what believers commemorate and celebrate when we come with grateful hearts to the Lord's Supper.

PAUSE TO REFLECT

It is not enough for those who profess faith in Christ to understand the institution of the Lord's Supper. We have a duty to partake of it. J. C. Ryle pointedly writes:

> Do we stay away from the Lord's Supper under a vague notion that there is no great necessity for receiving it? If we hold such an opinion, the sooner we give it up the better. A plain precept of God's own Son, is not to be trifled with in this way.—Do we stay away from the Lord's Supper because we are not fit to be communicants? If we do, let us thoroughly understand that we are not fit to die. Unfit for the Lord's table, we are unfit for heaven, unprepared for the judgment day, and not ready to meet God! Surely this is a most serious state of things.[3]

40.

Grief in a garden

◇◇◇◇◇◇◇◇◇◇◇◇◇◇◇◇◇◇◇◇◇◇◇◇◇◇◇◇◇◇◇◇◇◇◇◇

Matthew 26:36-46

On the night before our Lord was crucified, he went with his disciples to the Garden of Gethsemane. There he experienced unspeakable agony, as he poured out his heart to God. That experience culminated in Jesus being betrayed by Judas and taken into custody by the authorities.

Here is the question before us: what are we to take away from Jesus' grief in the garden? To put it another way, what are we to learn from it?

Jesus' humanity was real

When our Lord came to this earth, he added our humanity to his deity so that he was fully God and fully man. The God-man! He did not lay aside his deity, but he added true humanity. The deity was real, and the humanity was just as real.

It was the humanity of Jesus that shrank from the cross. We know what it is to embrace something with the mind or the spirit while shrinking from it with our flesh. This is our experience when we have surgery. Our minds tell us that the surgery is necessary and important, but we still dread it.

TIME OUT

William Hendriksen observes:

> Never shall we, who do not even know how our own soul and body interact, be able to grasp how the human nature of Christ, in these solemn moments, related itself toward the divine, or vice versa. To the intense suffering, experienced in Christ's human nature, was given infinite value by means of the union of this human to the divine nature, within the second person of the Holy Trinity.[1]

John Gill says of Christ's experience in Gethsemane:

> That there are two wills in Christ, human and divine, is certain; his human will, though in some instances, as in this, may have been different from the divine will, yet not contrary to it; and his divine will is always the same with his father's. This, as mediator, he engaged to do, and came down from heaven for that purpose, took delight in doing it, and has completely finished it.[2]

There is great consolation for us in the true humanity of Jesus. Because his humanity was genuine, he is able to sympathize with us in our humanity (Heb. 4:15). His humanity does not mean that he can sympathize with us; it is rather that he cannot help but sympathize with us.

Jesus' commitment to the cross was firm

We know that the Lord Jesus came to this earth with an appointment with the cross. He came here to die! This is the 'hour' to which he so often referred in John's Gospel.

We also know that he approached that appointment without flinching or wavering. His commitment to the cross was firm when he encountered Satan in the wilderness. The temptation to dismiss the cross was itself dismissed as Jesus sent Satan packing!

That commitment was in place when Jesus announced to his disciples on three occasions that he would die in Jerusalem. It was very much in place when he was transfigured with Moses and Elijah.

It was still firm when he observed his last supper with his disciples. He even went so far as to tell the disciples that Satan would come that very night to see if he could find in Jesus any unwillingness or reluctance to go to the cross, but he, Satan, would find nothing (John 14:30).

And Jesus always had an unruffled calm about him on every occasion that he spoke about the cross.

Then came Gethsemane, and all the commitment and calm seem to go right out of the window. Gethsemane, the garden where Jesus went with his disciples to pray just a few hours before his arrest, is the place where Jesus cried: 'O My Father, if it is possible, let this cup pass from Me...' (v. 39).

To many those words seem to suggest that Jesus got 'cold feet' at the last minute. He seems to throw overboard his firm resolution to go to the cross by making a last-ditch, frantic effort to avoid it. Gethsemane seems to be the place where the plan of salvation is hanging by a thread.

But that which, on the surface, seems to be Jesus wavering is really nothing of the sort. It is the opposite. It is really Jesus embracing the cross once again.

The author of Hebrews tells us that Jesus was 'perfected' by his experience in Gethsemane (5:9). That does not mean that Jesus had some flaw or deficiency that was corrected. Be clear about this: there was no flaw in Jesus!

It rather means that Jesus was equipped, fitted or qualified for a task. Brace yourself for a shocking statement: Jesus was not by nature qualified to perform the work of redemption! He had to take up certain equipment before he could perform that work. One piece of equipment was humanity. Jesus could not have saved us if he had not taken on our humanity. It was humanity that sinned, and only humanity could pay for the sin.

What piece of redemption's equipment did Jesus take up in Gethsemane? Complete identification with those he came to save! In the garden, he began to feel the pangs of God's judgement on our sins. There he began to experience the reality of God-forsakenness. And there, in his full identification with us, he cried out — as any doomed sinner would — 'let this cup pass'. In his human nature, he had to desire the cup of God's wrath against sin to pass, or he would not truly have been one of us.

If Jesus' experience in Gethsemane had to do with his complete identification with sinners, it, therefore, had nothing at all to do with Jesus suddenly being unwilling to go to the cross that he and the Father had planned before the world began. When Jesus died on the cross, it was not as the reluctant Son of a mean, unbending Father. Gethsemane was not Jesus' last-minute, desperate effort to persuade the Father to change his mind about the cross. It was Jesus fulfilling another requirement for his mission. As he emerged from the garden, Jesus emphatically said, 'Shall I not drink the cup which My Father has given Me?' (John 18:11).

When he emerged from Gethsemane, it was as one who could truly represent his people because he had fully and completely experienced their condemnation and cried their cry.

Grief in a garden

In his remarkable book, *The Cross He Bore*, Frederick S. Leahy rightly observes:

> In Gethsemane it was never a question whether the Saviour would obey or disobey. In Eden God asked, 'Adam, where are you?' In a sense the question was repeated in Gethsemane and this Adam did not try to hide; he had no need to; his whole response was clearly, 'Here am I!'[3]

The wrath of God is dreadful

We surely cannot leave Gethsemane without being deeply impressed by the awesome reality of the wrath of God against human sin. Jesus perfectly understood what he was facing on the cross. He would bear there the wrath of God in the place of his people so they would not have to bear that wrath themselves.

Now if the wrath of God was such that Jesus was terrified by it, how much more should we be terrified by it?

It is almost impossible these days to get people to take the wrath of God seriously. The whole thing has been decided! The poll has been conducted, the result is in and the wrath of God is out!

If the cross of Christ tells us anything, it tells us that the wrath of God is real, and we are fools to ignore it. Those who do ignore it will realize their folly at last as they cry for the rocks and mountains to fall on them and hide them from that wrath.

PAUSE TO REFLECT

Is there any hope for avoiding the wrath of God? There is! The hope is in the cross of Christ. If we want to be saved from the fire of

God's wrath, we must go to the place where it has already burned. It burned on the cross when Jesus died. If we will go there with true sorrow for our sins and with faith in what Jesus did, the wrath that burned there that day will never touch us.

41.

Betrayed, denied and
unjustly condemned

John 18:1-11,15-18,25-40

After Jesus prayed for his disciples in the Upper Room, he went with them to the Garden of Gethsemane where he engaged in fervent prayer to the Father as his disciples slept.

It was there in the garden that Jesus was seized and arrested by a delegation sent by 'the chief priests and Pharisees' and led by Judas Iscariot. From the garden, he was first taken to Annas then to Caiaphas and finally to Pilate. Three major truths stand out in these events.

Betrayed (vv. 1-11)

Jesus wasn't taken by surprise by the appearance of Judas and his detachment. He knew beforehand that they would be coming, and he knew exactly what lay ahead of him during the remaining hours of the night and throughout the next day. Knowing all this, he still 'went forward' (v. 4). What a glorious picture this is! Our Saviour, knowing all the terrible suffering at hand, willingly stepped forward to perform the work of redemption. Such was his inexpressible love for sinners!

When the mob identified Jesus of Nazareth as the one whom they were seeking, Jesus responded: 'I am He.' The men of the mob then 'drew back and fell to the ground.'

Jesus was, of course, fully God and fully man. His deity was, as it were, clothed in humanity. On this occasion, a beam of divinity flashed through Jesus' humanity and flattened these men. Those in the delegation sent to arrest Jesus experienced the glory of Jesus in the process but still refused to acknowledge his Lordship.

TIME OUT

Jesus stepped forward, identified himself and said of the disciples, 'Let these go their way.' We may picture him stepping between his arresters and his disciples. This provides a beautiful picture of his death on the cross. There he took our sins so we might freely go our way.

The 'cup' the Lord Jesus Christ was given to drink was the cross. It was given to him by the Father, and even though it contained anguish and agony we will never know, Jesus submitted to it.

The *Geneva Study Bible* states: 'This "cup" is the cup of the wine of God's wrath (Ps. 75:8; Is. 51:17; Jer. 25:15-17,27-38). The "cup" that Jesus chooses to drink is not merely death, but the wrath of God upon sin...' (p.1699).

Denied (vv. 15-18,25-27)

Given the opportunity to stand up and speak out for Christ, Simon Peter failed. Not once did he fail, not twice, but three times.

There was so much Simon could have said about the Lord Jesus Christ. He saw Jesus turn water into wine (John 2:1-11), and he saw him heal his mother-in-law of a high fever (Luke 4:38-39).

Simon Peter had seen Jesus feed five thousand with five barley loaves and two small fishes (John 6:1-13). He walked with Jesus on the stormy sea (John 6:15-21). He was on the Mount of Transfiguration when Jesus glistened with heavenly glory (Luke 9:27-35).

Peter had seen Jesus heal the lame (John 5:1-9) and the blind (John 9:1-7). He had even seen Jesus raise three people from the dead (Mark 5:39-42; Luke 7:11-15; John 11:43-44), one of whom had been dead four days (John 11:39).

In addition to all these things, Simon Peter, by his own admission, had heard in the words of Jesus the authentic ring of the message of eternal life (John 6:68).

Simon Peter could have talked about all these things and many, many more. He could have responded to the inquiry of the servant girl and those with her by affirming that he was a disciple of Jesus Christ and that he was glad to be in that number. He could have said that knowing Jesus was the supreme treasure of his life, and, no matter how many days he had remaining, nothing could ever come near the tremendous privilege that he had in those days in which he walked with the Lord Jesus.

Yes, that is what he could have said, but he did not. He had the opportunity to stand firm for Christ and bear witness, but he faltered and failed.

How shameful were Peter's three denials! He did not even attempt to soften them. He could have said, 'You have me confused with someone else', or, 'I don't know what you are talking about.' But he spat his denials out in the most unambiguous and emphatic way imaginable: 'I am not!' (vv. 17,25). Matthew tells us that Peter went so far as to lace his denials with cursing (Matt. 26:74).

Why did Simon Peter deny the one to whom he owed so much? Why did he refuse to confess his allegiance to the one who had rescued him from sin and so often thrilled him?

It comes down to one word — fear. Peter was afraid of what might happen to him if he professed allegiance to Jesus. By this time Jesus' predictions of his death (Matt. 16:21; 17:22-23; 20:17-19) must have finally fastened themselves in Peter's mind. He now knew that Jesus was going to die, and he was afraid that he would die with him if he admitted to being his disciple.

It wasn't long before Simon realized that he had feared the wrong thing. The enemies he regarded as a threat to his life could not hold a candle to the bitter disappointment that then flooded his soul (Mark 14:72; Luke 22:62).

Unjustly condemned (vv. 28-40)

Jesus is here before Pilate, the Roman governor of the Jewish state. The Sanhedrin had already condemned Jesus to death but they desperately wanted Pilate's approval for the death penalty. On occasions the Jews would execute someone without Rome's approval (Acts 7:54-60). Why, then, did they desire Rome's approval before executing Jesus? They may have feared his popularity would create a backlash against them if they did it on their own.

The more likely answer is that they wanted Jesus to be executed in the official Roman way — crucifixion. Crucifixion was designated in Scripture as a sign of God's curse (Deut. 21:23). If Jesus was crucified it would effectively terminate all talk of him being the Messiah. To their minds, a crucified Messiah was as impossible as a square circle.

John doesn't explicitly mention the charge the Jews were bringing against Jesus, but it is clear from Pilate's first question that the major charge was Jesus was setting himself up as a king in opposition to Caesar.

This charge shows us the huge hypocrisy of the religious leaders. They hated the Romans, and someone opposing Caesar was the least of their concerns. The reason they wanted Jesus crucified had nothing to do with a political kingdom, but with his claim to be the Son of God, a claim that was, to their minds, blasphemous. They knew, however, that religious issues would cut no ice with Pilate. So they re-fashioned the charge in terms that Pilate could not ignore, namely, that Jesus was a political revolutionary who was guilty of inciting rebellion against Rome.

In response to the question of whether he was a king, Jesus responded, saying in effect, 'Yes, but not the kind of king you think.'

Pilate and the Jews had one thing in common. When they thought about a king, they thought solely in terms of an earthly kingdom. Jesus made it clear that his kingdom was not of this earth. It is a spiritual kingdom that is built on the truth of God.

Pilate's initial conversation with Jesus convinced him that Jesus was innocent of the charges brought against him. From that moment he set about to release Jesus.

He first resorted to the Passover custom of releasing a prisoner (18:39-40). He asked the crowd to decide between Jesus and Barabbas, the latter probably being chosen because he was an unsavoury character.

When that ploy failed, Pilate decided to scourge Jesus and then bring him before the people (19:1-6). The scourge consisted of a leather whip with pieces of metal and bone. It was so terrible that many prisoners died in the process.

Few sights were more pathetic than that of a scourged man, but the hearts of the people were so hard that they were not even moved by this sickening sight.

Pilate had the authority to release Jesus. All he needed was the moral courage to do the right thing, but this he couldn't muster. When the Jews raised the possibility of him being disloyal to Caesar (19:12), Pilate showed his true colours. All concerns for justice evaporated as he caved in to the pressure. He washed his hands of the crime, but that water couldn't remove the cowardice of his heart.

In the face of Pilate's repeated attempts to release Jesus, the Jews finally blurted out the real reason they wanted him crucified: 'He made Himself the Son of God' (19:7).

This statement caused Pilate great consternation. Already the governor had been impressed by the words and demeanour of our Lord; he had never met a prisoner like him before. Was he indeed a god come to earth? Did he have supernatural powers?

These fearful thoughts drove Pilate to attempt to intimidate Jesus: 'Do You not know that I have power to crucify You, and power to release You?' (19:10).

Jesus calmly responded that Pilate had no power to do anything other than that which God had already determined should be done. The crucifixion was, therefore, at one and the same time the work of wicked men and the plan of God (Acts 2:23).

PAUSE TO REFLECT

In cutting off the servant's ear, Simon Peter was guilty of doing something Jesus had not commanded. Seeing the mob fall back from Jesus should have been enough to convince him that Jesus didn't need him swinging a sword. Had Jesus wanted to escape, one word from his mouth would have been more potent than all the disciples swinging swords.

In denying Jesus, Peter was guilty of *not* doing something Jesus had commanded. Jesus had made it clear that his church was to be built upon the confession that he is the Son of God (Matt. 16:13-18). Peter had the opportunity to confess but failed to do so.

Many churches today seem to have fallen into these same errors. They commit the first by seeking to advance the kingdom through means Christ has not commanded, and the second by failing to confess the true gospel.

42.

The day hell came out of heaven

Matthew 27:33-50; Mark 15:22-37

The public ministry of Jesus lasted approximately three and a half years. It ended when the religious leaders of Israel succeeded in getting the Roman government to crucify him.

There was no more agonizing way to die than crucifixion, and the Romans seemed to have employed it generously. It was not at all uncommon to see men hanging on crosses as one travelled the major thoroughfares of the day. The victims would often take three or four, or more, days to die.

Each of the four Gospels contains a gripping account of the crucifixion of Jesus, but, interestingly enough, each has little to say about the physical sufferings he endured. The reason is not hard to determine. The significance did not lie in Jesus being crucified. Lots of men were crucified in those days! It rather lay in what transpired between Jesus and God the Father during those hours of crucifixion. The Jesus who lived like no other, died like no other. On the cross, he actually offered himself as the sacrifice for human sin.

Matthew and Mark's accounts of the crucifixion are similar. Each speeds through several aspects of Jesus' death, dwelling more on the cruel mockery heaped upon him by the passers-by and the religious leaders. Little did these people realize that their mocking was fulfilling prophecy, and, therefore, adding proof to the very thing they were trying to deny, namely, that Jesus was indeed the Son of God.

The special feature in these two Gospels is their mention of these words from Jesus: 'My God, My God, why have You forsaken Me?' (Matt. 27:46; Mark 15:34). These words culminated three hours of deep, impenetrable darkness (Matt. 27:45; Mark 15:33).

Jesus spoke seven times from the cross, three times prior to this and three times following it. This is, then, the central word, and the word that takes us to the very heart of the meaning of his crucifixion.

TIME OUT

The other words Jesus spoke from the cross are:

- 'Father, forgive them, for they do not know what they do' (Luke 23:34).
- 'Assuredly, I say to you, today you will be with Me in Paradise' (Luke 23:43).
- To his mother: 'Woman, behold your son!' and to his disciple John: 'Behold your mother!' (John 19:26-27).
- 'I thirst!' (John 19:28).
- 'It is finished!' (John 19:30).
- 'Father, into Your hands I commit My spirit' (Luke 23:46).

Why did Jesus cry out about being forsaken? The answer lies in the penalty for sin and the nature of what Jesus was doing on the cross.

The penalty for sin

Human sin is an awesome and undeniable reality. What is sin? It is refusing to live according to God's commandments. It is the creature thumbing his nose in the face of his Creator and saying, 'I do not care how you want me to live. I will live the way I want.'

Sin always seems to be the simplest of matters to those who are doing the sinning. As far as they are concerned, it is merely a matter of God turning his head and looking the other way or saying with a shrug, 'Let's just forget it.' Sinners would like God to be like the indulgent parent who would rather ignore Junior's misdeeds than go through the trauma of dealing with them. Many these days have convinced themselves that this is in fact the way God is!

But the God of our fancies is not the real God. The true God cannot and will not regard sin as a trifling and negligible matter. Why does God take sin so seriously? The answer of the Bible is that he is holy (Exod. 15:11; Lev. 19:2; Deut. 32:4; Joshua 24:19; 1 Sam. 2:2; Isa. 6:3; Matt. 5:48; 1 Peter 1:15; 1 John 1:5; Rev. 4:8; 15:4).

He is not only free from sin himself, but he has the deepest aversion to it. The prophet Habakkuk states it graphically when he says to God, 'You are of purer eyes than to behold evil, and cannot look on wickedness' (Hab. 1:13).

God's holy nature requires him to pronounce judgement upon it. For God to ignore sin or refuse to punish it would require him to compromise with sin, and that would make him guilty of sin himself.

The Bible further tells us that this holy God has in fact pronounced sentence upon sinners. That sentence is nowhere stated more clearly than by the apostle Paul in 2 Thessalonians 1:9. There he says of sinners, 'These shall be punished with everlasting destruction from the presence of the Lord and from the glory of His power...'

Note especially that phrase 'from the presence of the Lord'. Sin separates from God. It separates us from fellowship with God in this life and in the life to come. In Matthew 25:41 we find that God will say to all those who appear before him in their sins, 'Depart from Me, you cursed, into the everlasting fire prepared for the devil and his angels.'

We only have to look at what happened after the first sin in history was committed. Adam and Eve hid themselves from God. They could not stand to be in the presence of the holy God (Gen. 3:8).

The experience of Adam and Eve tells us something else: God does not take delight in punishing sinners. So he came to seek them while they were hiding themselves.

So here is God: his holiness requires him to separate sinners from himself, and his grace compels him to forgive those sinners.

The pulsating, throbbing question of the ages is, then, how can the holy God both punish sinners and let them go free? To put it another way, the question is: how could God satisfy both the demands of his justice and the demands of his grace, when those demands seem to be conflicting and contradictory?

The nature of what Jesus was doing on the cross

The answer to that question is found in the cross of Christ. Jesus was not an ordinary man dying an ordinary death on that cross. That death on the cross was agreed upon by God the Father, God the Son and God the Holy Spirit before the world began. To be more specific, the three persons of the Godhead agreed that on the cross Jesus would receive the wrath of God in the stead of sinners. He would become sin for them. The apostle Paul puts it wonderfully. He says God 'made' Jesus 'to be sin for us, that we might become the righteousness of God in Him' (2 Cor. 5:21).

Enabled by the Spirit of God to look down the corridor of time and see the cross of Christ, the prophet Isaiah explained it by saying,

> And the LORD has laid on Him
> the iniquity of us all
>
> (Isa. 53:6).

Now we are in position to understand Jesus' crying: 'My God, My God, why have You forsaken Me?' Jesus was 'made' sin on the cross. The sins of others were laid on him. And the penalty for sin is separation from God.

For God to count Jesus guilty of the sins of others required him, God, to forsake Jesus because the penalty for sin is God-forsakenness.

If God had refused to truly forsake Jesus, he could not have counted him the substitute for sinners. That forsaking had to take place!

Some argue that God did not really forsake Jesus on the cross. It was rather a matter of Jesus feeling that he was forsaken. But if that had not been a true forsaking, there would have been no atonement for sinners.

Some explain Jesus' cry by merely saying he was quoting Psalm 22:1:

> My God, My God, why have You forsaken Me?
> Why are You so far from helping Me,
> And from the words of My groaning?

It is obvious that Jesus was quoting this psalm. But why? The answer is that this verse fit his situation. All of Psalm 22 is, in fact, a detailed prophecy of his death on the cross. By the way, this psalm also tells us why Jesus was forsaken on the cross, saying to God, 'But You are holy' (v. 3).

Jesus was forsaken because God's holiness demanded it. The glory of it all is that God only requires that the penalty for sin be paid once. If Jesus paid it, there is no penalty left for all those who take refuge in Jesus through faith. In other words, God cannot punish Jesus for my sins and then proceed to punish me as well. That would be unjust! If Jesus bore my God-forsakenness on the cross, there is, therefore, no such forsakenness for me to bear. If Jesus took my hell on the cross, there is no hell left for me, only heaven.

The cross was, then, God's way of satisfying both the demands of his justice and his grace. Justice looked upon the cross that day and said, 'I am satisfied. The penalty of God-forsakenness against sinners has been carried out.'

And grace looked upon that same cross and said, 'I am satisfied. Since Jesus bore the penalty of God-forsakenness for all who believe, they will never have to bear it themselves and can, therefore, be forgiven.'

If someone asks how Jesus could bear in a three-hour period of time an eternity's worth of wrath, we must admit that we are out of our depth. We can only say that as God in human flesh, Jesus had the capacity to bear an infinite amount of wrath in a finite amount of time. What a wonder!

Now we can understand why a thick veil of darkness was drawn around the land at the time of the crucifixion. It was a visible and outward manifestation of God's withdrawal from Jesus. The Bible says, 'God is light' (1 John 1:5). So if God withdrew from Jesus, darkness would be fitting.

PAUSE TO REFLECT

We do not appropriately handle Jesus' wail to his Father if we do not drill our hearts in the wonder of it. Jesus, who lived his whole life in communion with the Father, was separated from him. And the thing that should continually amaze and astound us is that he bore it all for undeserving sinners. Because Jesus cried, 'My God, My God, why have You forsaken Me?' those who believe in him will not have to cry it in eternity.

Let us know beyond any shadow of doubt that God will either find our sins on Jesus or on us. If he finds them on Jesus, we will never have to endure their penalty, but if he finds them on us, we must hear from God those tragic words: 'Depart from Me.'

W. Herschel Ford pointedly writes:

God spared not the Lord Jesus when He found sin on Him — the sin of others. Do you think He will spare you if you come up to judgment with your own sin on you? If He poured out His wrath on Him who bore no sin but ours, do you think He will hold back His wrath if you go on in sin and come to the end of the way with your sin still on you? But there is hope for you. 'He that believeth on the Son hath life, but he that believeth not the Son shall not see life, but the wrath of God abideth on him.'[1]

43.

The day glory came out of gloom

◇◇◇

Luke 23:50 - 24:43

The staggering assertion of each of the four Gospels is that Jesus of Nazareth did not stay in the grave in which he was placed. He arose! So the greatest death ever died culminated in the greatest victory ever achieved. Life sprang from death and glory from gloom. And the death knell sounded for death itself.

The prelude to the resurrection (23:50-56)

Luke is careful to set the stage for the resurrection. Such attention to detail! Joseph of Arimathea, a disciple of Jesus, emerges from the shadow of secrecy to boldly ask Pilate for the body of Jesus (vv. 50-52).

Having secured it, he takes it from the cross, wraps it in linen, and lays it in a tomb hewn from rock, a tomb which had never been used (v. 53).

Then women who had come with Jesus from Galilee went home to prepare 'spices and fragrant oils' for the body of Jesus, which they intended to apply on the day after the Sabbath (vv. 55-56).

Luke quite obviously wants us to know that Jesus was really dead and really buried. He does not want to leave room for some 'crackpot' explanation that Jesus had only temporarily passed out and was revived by the cool air of the tomb. Imagine it! The severely scourged and crucified Jesus, although weakened by loss of blood and dehydration, revives in the tomb, unwraps himself and rolls the massive stone away from the inside of the tomb!

By the way, it is quite a marvel that Jesus died as quickly as he did. Pilate was certainly amazed (Mark 15:44). Crucified men often lingered for several days before dying. Pilate and the religious leaders never realized that they were never in charge of things as they thought. They were on God's timetable, not their own, and God's was very precise. It called for the sacrifice to be complete on the day of Passover, the day on which lambs were sacrificed, and for resurrection on the first day of the week. Jesus could not tarry on the cross with resurrection awaiting! He had to move rapidly from one appointment to the other!

The evidence for the resurrection (24:1-43)

The curtain seems to have fallen on unrelieved tragedy when we come to the end of Luke 23. Jesus is dead and buried, and the tomb is sealed with a heavy stone. The religious leaders, who desired so desperately to get rid of Jesus, were undoubtedly congratulating themselves on their victory. They could now get back to practising their religion without his wretched interference.

But the curtain quickly lifts, and the truth begins to shine.

The bodily resurrection of Jesus is the cornerstone of the Christian faith. As the apostle Paul plainly teaches in

1 Corinthians 15, 'no resurrection' means 'no Christianity'. The resurrection proves Jesus to be God in human flesh. It also proves that God put his stamp of approval on what Jesus did on the cross. It shows that Jesus really did provide redemption for sinners by dying on that cross! The resurrection also guarantees that believers in Christ will themselves be raised from their graves to share in the eternal glory of the Lord.

Sceptics know the strategic importance of the resurrection, and they have spared no effort to discredit and dislodge it. Anticipating such attacks, Luke and the other Gospel writers give careful and detailed attention to the evidence for the resurrection.

TIME OUT

◇◇◇◇◇◇◇◇◇◇◇◇◇◇◇◇◇◇◇◇◇◇◇◇◇◇◇◇◇◇

H. D. A. Major observes:

Had the crucifixion of Jesus ended His disciples' experience of Him, it is hard to see how the Christian church could have come into existence. That church was founded on faith in the Messiahship of Jesus. A crucified messiah was no messiah at all. He was one rejected by Judaism and accursed of God.[1]

The stone (v. 2)

First, there was that stone. No small obstacle! Mark tells us that the women who went to the tomb on the first day of the week vexed themselves with the matter of rolling that stone away (Mark 16:3). Matthew lets us know that a Roman guard was also posted at the tomb to make sure no one removed the stone and stole the body (Matt. 27:62-66).

But there was no need for concern. The heaviness of the stone and the presence of the guard were ineffective deterrents.

When the women arrived, the stone was already removed and the guards were in a stupor (Matt. 28:4).

The missing body (vv. 3-4a)

Then there was the fact that the body was missing. It is perplexing that the women were 'greatly perplexed' by this. Jesus had plainly said on more than one occasion that he would arise, but his disciples never took it in. This shows how slow we are in comprehending spiritual truth. We are like the dog who, when someone points to a bone, sniffs the finger instead of the bone.

The missing body should have been conclusive proof for the women. The disciples, with a Roman guard present and with their own fear of the religious leaders, would not have attempted to steal the body. And the enemies of Jesus would certainly not have stolen it. The only explanation for it was resurrection.

The angels (vv. 4b-8)

Luke joins Matthew and Mark in making mention of the angels at the tomb, who were stationed there to explain to the women what had taken place. The women must have winced at this word of rebuke from the angels: 'Why do you seek the living among the dead?' (v. 5).

We do not seek the living in a cemetery, but here these women were standing at a tomb despite the fact that Jesus had promised his own resurrection.

The linen wrappings (v. 12)

When Simon Peter received the news of the empty tomb and the missing body, he ran to see for himself. It was just as the women said, but he also took note of the cloths in which the body of Jesus had been wrapped. There had to be something about those cloths that was particularly convincing. It would seem that they retained the shape of the body although the body was gone. Just as Jesus would later enter a room without opening the door, so he had evidently gone through those wrappings!

The appearances of the risen Christ (vv. 13-43)

Luke records two appearances of Jesus on the day of the resurrection. The first was to two disciples, with whom he walked from Jerusalem to Emmaus (vv. 13-35). The second was to his disciples back in Jerusalem (vv. 36-43). The other Gospels include other accounts of appearances as well, and the apostle Paul mentions one appearance to five hundred people (1 Cor. 15:6). A rather convincing number of witnesses!

PAUSE TO REFLECT

We need not be in doubt about the resurrection of Jesus. The evidence is strong and overwhelming. The question is whether we understand the implications of it. One has to do with the person of Jesus. His resurrection from the grave leaves no room for discussion or debate. Jesus Christ is Lord of all. We can either acknowledge that in this life, or we can acknowledge it when we finally meet him face to face; but all will eventually acknowledge it. Paul says every knee will bow and every tongue will confess that Jesus is Lord (Phil. 2:9-11).

Another has to do with the future of those who belong to Jesus. The Lord Jesus pointedly stated that his resurrection would guarantee the same for all his people (John 14:19).

44.

The risen Lord meeting

the needs of his people

John 20:14-21,24-29

In addition to assuring us of the reality of the resurrection of Jesus, these verses lay before us some of the implications of it. Here we find Mary sorrowing outside the tomb, the disciples quivering in fear, and Thomas in the grip of doubt. But the resurrected Christ turned sorrow to joy, fear to peace and doubt to certainty.

This lesson is extremely important for us because sorrow, fear and doubt still afflict the people of God today. But the similarity doesn't end there. As the truth of the resurrection dispelled those emotions on that first Easter so it can dispel the same emotions today.

The risen Lord dispelling sorrow (vv. 14-18)

The tragedy of Mary's sorrow (vv. 14-15)

Verse 11 tells us Mary Magdalene (v. 11) stood weeping outside the tomb of Jesus. This was tragic because Mary, out of whom Jesus had cast seven demons (Mark 16:9), should have known Jesus had the power to conquer death as he had promised, but she refused to think of either his power or his promises. To her, Jesus' death was final and irreversible, and there was nothing to do but sob. She wept both out of unbelief and out of her great love for Jesus.

This tragedy was compounded by the fact that she looked into the tomb and saw two angels there and no body (vv. 11-12). This was powerful evidence that Jesus had indeed risen, but Mary assumed that these angels were mere men and that they had stolen the body! It seems as if she was looking hard for reasons not to believe.

She persisted in her unbelief when the Lord Jesus himself appeared to her. Supposing him to be the gardener, she asked him to show her where he had hidden the body (vv. 14-15).

The wonderful grace of the risen Lord (v. 16)

The Lord Jesus came to Mary in her sorrow and wiped it all away by simply calling her name. Her unbelief made her deserving of a stern rebuke, but the Lord Jesus did not rebuke her. His mere presence was rebuke enough!

The proper response to the risen Lord (vv. 17-18)

Mary at first responded to the Lord by apparently wrapping her arms around him as if she would never let him go. But after a word from Jesus, she released him and went to tell his disciples. Let us learn from this that we do not respond properly to the truth of Christianity by simply basking in it, but rather by trumpeting it all around.

The risen Lord dispelling fear (vv. 19-21)

The reason for their fear (v. 19a)

This account next calls our attention to the Lord appearing to his troubled, trembling disciples. These men knew that the same authorities that had ripped Jesus away from them and crucified him would not hesitate to eliminate them as well.

The treatment of their fear (vv. 19b-20)

The disciples weren't in the clutches of fear for long. The Lord Jesus suddenly appeared in their midst without making use of the door (which they would probably have refused to answer). He immediately said, 'Peace be with you' (v. 19) and showed them his hands and side (v. 20).

A simple syllogism must have gone sailing through the minds of the 'trembling ten' (minus the absent Thomas) when they heard these words and saw the hands and side of Jesus.

Major premise — If Jesus is here, he must have risen from the grave;

Minor premise — If Jesus has risen, he must be Lord of all;

Conclusion — If Jesus is Lord of all there is no need to fear the Jews or anyone else.

An assurance for the future (v. 21)

The Lord Jesus was not content to simply allay his disciples' fear of the Jews. He wanted them to understand that they would soon be ministering to the very men of whom they had been so afraid.

The knowledge of his resurrection and the gift of the Holy Spirit were all they would need to become faithful witnesses.

The risen Lord dispelling doubt (vv. 24-29)

Thomas was not present when the Lord Jesus appeared to his fearful disciples (v. 24). When he did appear, he found them talking excitedly about what they had seen. He was not impressed. He declared that he would not believe until he could actually put his finger into the print of the nails in the hands and thrust his hand into the spear wound in the side of the risen Lord (v. 25).

After eight days, Thomas had his chance. Jesus appeared again to the disciples with Thomas present and essentially said, 'Thomas, do what you have said you would do' (vv. 26-27).

Thomas didn't live up to his bold words. The fact that Jesus quoted his words precisely could mean only one thing: Jesus knew that he, Thomas, had spoken them. How could Jesus have known what he said if he, Jesus, were not the risen Lord? So Thomas didn't feel but fell. He fell at the feet of Jesus and cried: 'My Lord and my God!'

TIME OUT

◇◇◇◇◇◇◇◇◇◇◇◇◇◇◇◇◇◇◇◇◇◇◇◇◇◇◇◇◇◇◇

Thomas' is one of several confessions of faith in John's Gospel:

John the Baptist (1:29)
Nathanael (1:49)
The Samaritans (4:42)
Simon Peter (6:69)
Martha (11:27)
John, the author of the Gospel (20:31)

TIME OUT

In addition to these, the Gospel also reports Jesus' own testimony about his identity (10:36).

PAUSE TO REFLECT

Christians are not immune from sorrow, fear and doubt. The devil is ever eager to assure us that these things prove our Christianity to be untrue, or, at the very least, prove us not to be Christians.

As always, our defence is in looking to the Lord Jesus. The fact that he tenderly dealt with his deficient disciples tells us that he does not write us off because we are weak and faltering. And the proofs that he gave of his resurrection mean our faith is well grounded. When we feel sorrow, fear or doubt, let us look to the resurrection and let us know that there is strength for our present and hope for our future.

The question is not whether we experience sorrow, fear and doubt. It is rather whether we know what to do with them. Let's take them to the resurrection!

45.

Kind grace for weak

◇◇

and failing men

◇◇◇◇◇◇◇◇◇◇◇◇◇◇◇◇◇◇◇◇◇◇◇◇◇◇◇◇◇◇◇◇◇◇◇◇

John 21

The appearances of the risen Christ to his disciples certainly constitute one of the most profound and convincing evidences for his resurrection. When we put these appearances alongside the other evidences, we realize that we need not be in doubt about this staggering and monumental event. Faith's footing is sure.

There is much about these appearances that is fascinating. Perhaps the most gripping feature is the wonderful grace and kindness that the Lord Jesus expressed toward his disciples, all of whom were very weak and failing.

We never see that kind grace more pointedly demonstrated than in this chapter of John's Gospel. Here Jesus provides reassurance for seven of his disciples and special reassurance for Simon Peter. And the Lord Jesus displays that same grace to his people today.

Reassurance for seven disciples

The fishing disciples (v. 3b)

Seven of Jesus' disciples decided to go fishing. This has sparked considerable debate among commentators. Some think these men were turning their backs on their calling to discipleship and were returning to their former livelihood. It would not be surprising if this were the case. These men had reason to believe that Jesus would want nothing more to do with them. They probably believed that they had hopelessly compromised their standing as disciples by failing to stay with Jesus when he was arrested and crucified.

Other commentators insist that there was nothing wrong in these men going fishing. They point out these men had been riding an emotional roller coaster for several days and were now seeking some refreshment and relaxation while awaiting further orders from Jesus. These commentators commend the disciples for occupying their time with meaningful labour instead of sitting in idleness.

The futility of the disciples in their fishing may very well have been intended by Jesus to remind them of a previous fishing failure which ended with them forsaking all to follow Jesus (Luke 5:1-11). It also foreshadowed the large 'catch' of men and women in which they, the disciples, would participate on the Day of Pentecost (Acts 2:40-41).

TIME OUT
◇◇◇◇◇◇◇◇◇◇◇◇◇◇◇◇◇◇◇◇◇◇◇◇◇◇◇◇◇◇◇◇◇

The fact that the disciples caught no fish that night was no accident: it was planned in order to give these men an object lesson. Glyn Owen observes: 'Our Lord wanted to teach them that life outside his will is utterly futile. He graciously, firmly showed

TIME OUT

◇◇◇◇◇◇◇◇◇◇◇◇◇◇◇◇◇◇◇◇◇◇◇◇◇◇◇

his security-seeking followers that the very best skill, exercised in the most familiar of circumstances, is no guarantee of success, outside his will. The fishing failure was love's way of showing that there are as many perils in withdrawing from the Lord as there may be in going on with him.[1]

The reassuring Saviour (vv. 4-13)

The assurance provided by the multitude of fish (vv. 4-8). As on the occasion of their first fishing failure, Jesus arrived on the scene and instructed them regarding their fishing. And once again they complied with Jesus' instruction and met with huge success (Luke 5:1-11). The fish, like the disciples themselves, were in the hands of the sovereign Lord.

Once the disciples realized that the stranger on the shore was Jesus (v. 7), they undoubtedly called to mind the events described in Luke 5. And we can also be sure that they were quick to reason that if Jesus wanted them to follow him when he first helped them with their fishing, he must have helped them on this occasion because he wants them to continue following him. The Lord's calling had not been negated by their failure.

At the same moment they realized that Jesus still had work for them to do, another realization must have flooded in upon them — that the same Lord who was sufficient for them in the work of fishing would prove to be sufficient for them in the work of fishing for men. They must have further realized that they could not possibly succeed on their own but must depend totally upon his strength.

The assurance provided by the breakfast (vv. 9-13). It would not be surprising if these seven disciples found Jesus' invitation to breakfast to be even more reassuring than the catch of fish. In that culture, an invitation to eat involved far more than eating. It was also — even as it is today — an invitation to fellowship and communion. The very Lord whom they had failed still desired to enjoy fellowship with them!

This passage begins with the disciples on the sea and the Lord Jesus on the shore. The disciples make their way to shore in different ways and once there find food prepared and enter into communion with Jesus.

We are even now on the sea of life. It is often a turbulent sea, and we are tossed about. But our Christ stands on the heavenly shore, overseeing our labours and assuring us that his strength is sufficient for us.

One day we will ourselves make it to heaven's shore, where he will personally receive us. And there we will find a banquet spread before us such as we have never seen. Most of all, thank God, we shall engage in sweet communion with Christ, communion that will never be broken or destroyed.

Reassurance for Simon Peter (vv. 15-17)

Simon Peter had failed in a most shocking and grievous manner. On the night before Jesus was crucified, Peter denied his faith in him and any association with him.

Simon denied Jesus, even though he swore he would not. He denied with great emphasis and vehemence, even resorting to profanity in the process. Furthermore, he denied, not once or twice, but three times.

The passage before us presents incredibly good news for all those saints of God who have trodden or are treading the path of denial that Simon Peter walked: the Lord Jesus Christ will never let his people go. Here we find him pursuing Simon and restoring him to fellowship with himself and to usefulness in his kingdom. Thank God for pursuing and restoring grace!

The restoration of Peter was worked out against a backdrop specifically designed to remind him of the denials. These had occurred as Peter warmed himself by the fire (John 18:17-18, 25-27), and here he finds himself face to face with Jesus beside the fire (v. 9). Three times Peter had denied the Lord, and here he is asked three times if he truly loves the Lord.

We should also note that Jesus addressed him as 'Simon' instead of 'Peter', which means 'rock'. Peter had failed to live up to his name.

The first question included the phrase 'more than these' and is probably a reference to the other disciples. It reminded Simon Peter of his boast that he would not forsake Jesus even if all the others did (Mark 14:29).

The second and third questions exclude the comparison and simply ask Simon Peter if he could honestly affirm love for Christ. Some have made a great deal of the fact that he and Jesus used different words for love, and other interpreters point out that the two Greek verbs for love are often used interchangeably in classical Greek literature.

Jesus' dealing with Simon Peter in these verses ought to encourage us. No matter how his people fail, the Lord is willing to forgive and restore.

The Lord demands sacrificial service from Simon Peter (vv. 15-19)

It is never enough simply to profess love for Christ. True love will always reveal itself in action. Therefore, after each of Peter's affirmations of love the Lord said, 'Feed My lambs,' or 'Feed My sheep.'

Some think Jesus had in mind different age groups within the church and was calling Simon Peter was to manifest his love toward the Lord by caring for the Lord's people whether they be young believers (lambs) or mature believers (sheep). Others think Jesus was looking at his people from different angles: while they are like weak lambs and straying sheep, they are always the objects of his affection.

This much is plain: there is a distinct and definite connection between loving Christ and loving his people. Commitment to Christ always involves commitment to his church. If we do not have the latter, we have no right to conclude that we have the former.

Love to Christ not only manifests itself in terms of sacrificial service but also in suffering. For Peter this would mean eventual martyrdom. God does not call all his people to die for Christ, but he does call them to suffer for him (Phil. 1:29; 2 Tim. 3:12).

The Lord provides focus for Simon Peter (vv. 20-25)

When Simon Peter heard what lay ahead for him, he turned to John and said, 'What about this man?' (v. 21). The Lord's revelation of martyrdom for Simon made him wonder if his dear friend, John, would share that fate. But, as Jesus made plain in his answer, the matter was none of Simon's business (v. 22).

This reminds us of how very easy it is for us to concern ourselves with matters that the Lord has not chosen to reveal, rather than with those things that he has.

William Hendriksen notes:

There is work to be done. There are souls to be reached. There is a task to be accomplished. Let Peter rivet all his attention upon this! Some people are always asking questions. They are asking so many questions that their real mission in life fails to receive the proper amount of interest and energy.[2]

PAUSE TO REFLECT

The seven disciples in this chapter had all failed Jesus in one way or another, but he refused to let them go. His people are in the grip of relentless grace. Grace has saved us, and grace will see us through this life and get us safely home.

> Thro' many dangers, toils, and snares,
> I have already come;
> 'Tis grace hath bro't me safe thus far,
> And grace will lead me home

(John Newton).

46.

The ascension of Jesus

Acts 1:10-11; 2:33-36

I know a neglected child. It is heart-breaking. This child is one of many children. He is just as intelligent, gifted and beautiful as all the other children. But he does not receive the same amount of attention. It is sad.

What is the name of this family? It is the 'Doctrine' family. And what is the name of the child? It is 'Ascension'.

Yes, I am saying that the ascension of Christ into heaven is one of the most neglected doctrines of the Christian faith. The incarnation of Christ is not neglected: we celebrate it at Christmas. The crucifixion is not neglected: we celebrate it on Good Friday. The resurrection is not neglected: we celebrate it at Easter.

But it is not so with the ascension. Although we have Ascension Day on the Christian calendar, it receives little or no attention. Check it out for yourself. When did you last hear a sermon on the ascension of Christ?

This neglect of the ascension is sad because our neglect robs us of comfort and assurance that we desperately need in these days.

Let us give this doctrine its due. Let us seek to understand it. And let us resolve that we will never again neglect it.

The ascension of Jesus speaks to us about three things of vital importance.

He is our reigning King

After he arose from the grave, the Lord Jesus spent forty days with his disciples. During this time he furnished them with 'many infallible proofs' of his resurrection (Acts 1:3). When this period was over, he ascended to the Father in heaven (Acts 1:9).

The Scriptures make it clear that Jesus was received there by the Father. He was given a seat at the right hand of God (Eph. 1:20; Col. 3:1; Heb. 12:2).

This is the seat of honour. Completely satisfied with Jesus' work of redemption, God the Father has, in the words of Paul, 'highly exalted Him and given Him the name which is above every name' (Phil. 2:9).

We must not place the reign of Christ entirely in the future. He is reigning now.

On the Day of Pentecost, the apostle Peter stood before the thousands gathered in Jerusalem to proclaim that Jesus began to reign as soon as he was seated at the Father's right hand. For proof of his assertion, Peter cited the coming of the Holy Spirit (Acts 2:33).

The Holy Spirit is, then, the gift of the risen, reigning Christ to his followers to enable them to carry out his work in the world.

Do we sufficiently realize that Jesus Christ is now reigning from the throne of heaven? He is not frantically running around heaven in a panic. He is not anxiously fretting over whether he will be able to bring all things to their appointed end. He reigns even now as Lord over all!

Sober reflection on this truth will do wonders for us. For one thing, it will cause us to stop fretting and worrying over events and circumstances that are out of our control. They are not out of his control! Our Christ reigns!

He is our interceding and sympathizing Priest

From that seat of authority, Jesus Christ also continues his work as our great High Priest.

When he went to the cross, he did so in the capacity of the High Priest of his people. There he sacrificed himself for their sins. He was both the offering Priest and the sacrifice that was offered!

Now at the right hand of God, he intercedes. When one truly comes to God the Father in repentance and faith, the Lord Jesus essentially says to the Father, 'I have done all that is necessary for him to be forgiven and received.'

TIME OUT

He took his meritorious blood,
And rose above the skies,
And in the presence of his God,
Presents his sacrifice.
His intercession must prevail,
With such a glorious plea
My cause can never, never fail,
For Jesus died for me.

(author unknown).

The author of Hebrews also tells us that Jesus expresses great sympathy as he cares for the needs of his people (Heb. 4:14-16).

He is our guaranteeing forerunner (Heb. 6:20)

There's yet another implication of the ascension, and it is one very few seem to ponder. When Jesus ascended to the Father, he took our humanity back into glory with him. Here again we see the marvel of his grace. When he took our humanity, it wasn't just for the years he was here on earth. It was for ever.

The Lord Jesus didn't cease to be a man after he went back into heaven. He now has a glorified body, but it is still a body.

In his hymn, 'Crown Him with Many Crowns', Matthew Bridges writes:

Crown Him the Lord of love;
Behold His hands and side,
Those wounds, yet visible above,
In beauty glorified:
All hail, Redeemer, hail!
For Thou hast died for me:
Thy praise and glory shall not fail
Throughout eternity.

And the fact that he is in heaven now as our forerunner guarantees that all who belong to him will follow him into heaven in the same kind of body he now has.

He is our returning Saviour

After they saw the Lord Jesus taken into heaven, the disciples found themselves in the presence of two angels, who said, 'Men of Galilee, why do you stand gazing up into heaven? This same Jesus, who was taken up from you into heaven, will so come in like manner as you saw Him go into heaven' (Acts 1:11).

Many centuries have come and gone since that promise was given, but it is still in effect, and we should not doubt it for a single moment.

If Jesus ascended into heaven, he is God. And if he is God, he cannot lie (Titus 1:2; Heb. 6:18). And if he cannot lie, he will keep the promise he gave to those disciples through his angels.

On the day that he comes, he will escort all God's people into heaven itself. The dead will be raised from their graves. The living will be 'caught up' to meet him in the air (1 Thess. 4:13-18). All will receive those glorified bodies that we noted earlier.

Then we will finally begin to understand the greatness of our Saviour's redeeming work, and we will praise our incarnate, crucified, risen and ascended Lord with hearts bursting with gratitude.

PAUSE TO REFLECT

The kingship of Christ confronts all of us with a most urgent and probing question: will we own him as our king?

Michael Horton writes:

When Britain's sovereigns are crowned, a solemn question is asked of their subjects: 'I present to you your undoubted king. Will you do him homage?'

In unison, Westminster Abbey's throng cheers in (it is hoped) triumphant affirmation.

In similar fashion both Old and New Testaments offer to us our King and demand our response: 'Kiss the Son' (Ps. 2:12), for at his name every knee is bowed (Phil. 2:10).[1]

The Bible makes our option clear. We can either bow before Christ now and confess the truth about him, or we can bow in eternity in his presence. But we all will bow. Those who wait till eternity to do their bowing will find themselves driven from his presence into eternal woe.

Notes

Chapter 2 – The boy Jesus in the temple

1. Matthew Poole, *A Commentary on the Holy Bible*, MacDonald Publishing Company, vol. iii, p.200.
2. John Blanchard lists these and other facts about Jesus in *Meet the Real Jesus*, Evangelical Press, pp.11-13.
3. R. C. Sproul, *The Glory of Christ*, P&R Publishing, p.51.

Chapter 3 – The Trinity at the Jordan

1. William Hendriksen, *New Testament Commentary: Matthew*, Baker Book House, p.217.

Chapter 5 – A question

1. Leon Morris, *The Gospel According to John*, Wm B. Eerdmans Publishing Co., p.171.

Chapter 6 – The first sign

1. J. C. Ryle, *Expository Thoughts on John*, The Banner of Truth Trust, vol. i, p.102.
2. As above, p.94.
3. Warren Wiersbe, *The Bible Exposition Commentary*, Victor Books, vol. i, p.292.

Chapter 7 – Cleansing the temple

1. William Hendriksen, *New Testament Commentary: John*, Baker Book House, p.124.
2. A. W. Pink, *Exposition of the Gospel of John*, Zondervan Publishing House, p.99.
3. Bruce Milne, *The Message of John*, Inter-Varsity Press, pp.70-71.

Chapter 8 – A teacher goes to night school

1. Ryle, *John*, vol. i, p.125.
2. William Barclay, *The Daily Study Bible: The Gospel of John*, The Westminster Press, vol. i, p.114.
3. Ryle, *John*, vol. i, p.123.
4. Gordon J. Keddie, *An EP Study Commentary: John*, Evangelical Press, vol. i, p.132.
5. Matthew Henry, *Matthew Henry's Commentary*, Fleming H. Revell Company, vol. v, p.885.

Chapter 9 – Good news for an outcast

1. Ryle, *John*, vol. i, p.205.
2. James Montgomery Boice, *The Gospel of John*, Zondervan Publishing House, p.248.
3. Keddie, *John*, vol. i, pp.187-88.

Notes

Chapter 10 – Lessons from a troubled man

1. Cited by Boice, *John*, p.294.
2. Ryle, *John*, vol. i, p.255.
3. As above, p.256.

Chapter 13 – The mysterious and the plain

1. Ryle, *John*, vol. i, p.267.
2. S. G. DeGraaf, *Promise and Deliverance*, Paideia Press, vol. iv, p.45.

Chapter 15 – Great gratitude

1. J. C. Ryle, *Expository Thoughts on Luke*, The Banner of Truth Trust, vol. i, p. 237.
2. As above, p.238.
3. As above, p.242.
4. William Hendriksen, *New Testament Commentary: Luke*, Baker Book House, p.109.
5. Henry, *Commentary*, vol. v, p.655.
6. Alexander Maclaren, *Expositions of Holy Scripture*, Baker Book House, vol. ix, p.197.
7. As above.

Chapter 16 – A man hopelessly possessed

1. Maclaren, *Expositions*, vol. viii, p.177.
2. D. M. Lloyd-Jones, *Evangelistic Sermons*, The Banner of Truth Trust, p.111.
3. As above.

Chapter 17 – A woman hopelessly ill

1. *Family Treasury of Sunday Reading*, Rev. Andrew Cameron, ed., Thomas Nelson and Sons, p.159.
2. Willliam L. Lane, *The Gospel According to Mark*, William B. Eerdmans Publishing Company, p.193.
3. William Hendriksen, *New Testament Commentary: Mark*, Baker Book House, p.209.

Chapter 18 – A father hopelessly bereaved

1. R. C. H. Lenski, *The Interpretation of St Mark's Gospel*, Augsburg Publishing House, p.227.
2. Charles R. Erdman, *The Gospel of Mark*, The Westminster Press, p.89.

Chapter 19 – A shepherd for the multitude

1. Boice, *John*, p.382.

Chapter 20 – Who can this be?

1. J. C. Ryle, *Expository Thoughts on the Gospels: Mark*, The Banner of Truth Trust, p.84.

Chapter 24 – The transfiguration of Jesus

1. R. C. Sproul, *Essential Truths of the Christian Faith*, Tyndale House Publishers, Inc., p.93.
2. Charles R. Erdman, *The Gospel of Matthew*, The Westminster Press, p.136.
3. Sproul, *Essential Truths*, p.93.
4. R. Kent Hughes, *Preaching the Word: Mark*, Crossway Books, vol. ii, pp.15-16.
5. J. Glyn Owen, *From Simon to Peter*, Evangelical Press, p.147.

6. As above.

Chapter 25 – A boy suffering from seizures

1. Ryle, *Mark*, p.182.
2. Hendriksen, *Mark*, p.347.

Chapter 26 – A gracious invitation

1. St Augustine, *The Confessions of St Augustine*, Zondervan Publishing House, p.7.

Chapter 27 – Truth from a trap

1. Keddie, *John*, vol. i, p.312.
2. S. G. DeGraaf, *Promise and Deliverance*, vol. iv, p.61.
3. Keddie, *John*, p.313.

Chapter 28 – Two healings for one man

1. Ryle, *John*, vol. ii, pp.152-53.
2. Hendriksen, *John*, vol. ii, p.76.
3. Henry, *Commentary*, vol. v, pp.1012-13.
4. Charles R. Erdman, *The Gospel of John*, The Westminster Press, pp.87-88.

Chapter 29 – Three would-be disciples

1. Leon Morris, *The Gospel According to St Luke*, Wm B. Eerdmans Publishing Co., p.180.

Chapter 31 – Ten lepers cleansed

1. *Holman Bible Dictionary*, Trent C. Butler, ed, Holman Bible Publishers, pp.872-73.

2. Wiersbe, *Commentary*, vol. i, p.245.
3. Douglas J. W. Milne, *Let's Study Luke*, The Banner of Truth Trust, p.264.

Chapter 33 – Kingship demonstrated

1. Hendriksen, *Luke*, p.853.

Chapter 34 – Kingship clarified

1. DeGraaf, *Promise and Deliverance*, vol. iii, p.423.

Chapter 35 – An astonishing proof

1. Os Guinness, *The Dust of Death*, InterVarsity Press, p.385.
2. As above.

Chapter 36 – A loving act from a loving heart

1. G. Campbell Morgan, *The Gospel According to John*, Fleming H. Revell Company, p.207.
2. As above, p.208.
3. Hendriksen, *John*, p.180.
4. Cited by Clarence Edward Macartney, 'Come before Winter', *20 Centuries of Great Preaching*, Word Books, vol. ix, p.137.
5. Henry, *Commentary*, vol. v, p.1070.
6. Morgan, *John*, p.208.

Chapter 38 – Jesus washes the disciples' feet

1. R. V. G. Tasker, *The Gospel According to St John*, Wm B. Eerdmans Publishing Company, p.155.
2. Boice, *John*, pp.880-81.

Notes

Chapter 39 – One meal ended, another begun

1. Hendriksen, *Luke*, p.961.
2. As above, pp.960-61.
3. Ryle, *Luke*, vol. ii, p.398.

Chapter 40 – Grief in a garden

1. Hendriksen, *Matthew*, p.918.
2. John Gill, *Exposition of the Old & New Testaments*, The Baptist Standard Bearer, vol. vii, p.335.
3. Frederick S. Leahy, *The Cross He Bore*, The Banner of Truth Trust, pp.9-10.

Chapter 42 – The day hell came out of heaven

1. W. Herschel Ford, *Seven Simple Sermons on the Saviour's Last Words*, Zondervan Publishing House, pp.55-56.

Chapter 43 – The day glory came out of gloom

1. Cited by Josh McDowell, *The New Evidence that Demands a Verdict*, Thomas Nelson Publishers, p.255.

Chapter 45 – Kind grace for weak and failing men

1. Owen, *From Simon to Peter*, p.239.
2. Hendriksen, *John*, p.491.

Chapter 46 – The ascension of Jesus

1. Michael Horton, *We Believe*, Word Publishing, Nashville, p.129.

Other books by the author...

Foundations
for the faith

A
step-by-step
guide to
the Gospel of John

The Gospel of John may very well be the best loved of all the books of the Bible. Written at a time when many false teachers were challenging the basic facts of the gospel, John produced this grand and glorious Gospel that its readers 'may believe that Jesus is the Christ, the Son of God'.

As many today seem to be following that same path of unbelief as those in John's day, Roger Ellsworth has written this easy-to-read and thoroughly biblical work, in which he takes us through the whole Gospel, reiterating the truth that Jesus truly is God's Son. He encourages us to hold fast to the truths that John taught, and stirs us up to read more deeply into the Scriptures that we might have a closer walk with the one who demonstrated his lordship in his own life, death and resurrection.

This work also contains a memory verse for each study, and 'Digging Deeper' and 'Action' sections so that it is suitable for use in Sunday school or study classes. It is divided into fifty-two chapters to make it ideal for a weekly study group to cover the entire Gospel in a year.

Foundations for the faith, Roger Ellsworth, ISBN-13: 978-0-85234-615-0, 352 pages, EP Books.

The God of all comfort

Reflections in Isaiah

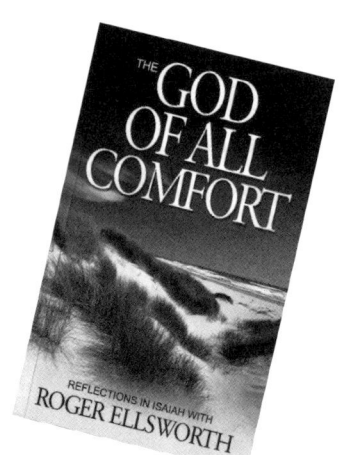

The prophecy of Isaiah may seem to be a strange and even difficult place from which to write a book about comfort, but the final twenty-seven chapters are rich beyond compare for those needing encouragement and help.

Written for the people of Israel while they were in captivity in Babylon, the prophecy was given to encourage them that things would not always be so difficult. Despite all their feelings to the contrary God had not abandoned them and the promises he had made to them in the past had not been rendered invalid by their disobedience. He loved his people and would be faithful to them.

Yet this is anything but a book about the past. The picture here is one with which we will all identify. Our world today can seem just like Babylon, with God's people being assailed from all sides. There are times when our faith fails and our spirits flag. We wonder whether our failings are so great that God has left us to our own devices. We ask ourselves where our problems will end, and whether God knows what he is doing after all.

In *The God of all comfort* Roger Ellsworth assures us that God knows exactly what he is doing and is in complete control of every situation, even when he appears not to be.

The God of all comfort, Roger Ellsworth, ISBN-13: 978-0-85234-549-8, 288 pages, EP Books.

The Bible
book
by book

The Bible book by book provides a complete overview of the Bible, divided into fifty-two chapters, which is ideal for use as a resource for a group Bible study or on an individual basis. It covers every book of the Bible, giving both its historical and spiritual significance, and shows how each individual book fits into God's perfect plan for his people throughout history. ISBN-13: 978-0-85234-486-6, 432 pages.

31 great
chapters of
the OT

We know that reading our Bibles is vital in developing our faith and our relationship with God, but where do we start? We could read the Bible from beginning to end, or read through a particular book; but another excellent method is delving into the Bible's best-known and best-loved chapters. Here, in just thirty-one days, Roger Ellsworth takes us on a whirlwind journey to the mountaintops of the Old Testament, presenting the foundational truths of Scripture. ISBN-13: 978-0-85234-686-0, 256 pages.

What the Bible teaches about…

What the Bible teaches about angels
ISBN-13: 978-0-85234-617-4, 128 pages

What the Bible teaches about heaven
ISBN-13: 978-0-85234-662-4, 128 pages

What the Bible teaches about Christian parenting
ISBN-13: 978-0-85234-648-8, 112 pages

All published by EP Books.